NATURAL RESOURCE MANAGEMENT

Volume 11

# The Politics of Industrial Agriculture

# Full list of titles in the set
## NATURAL RESOURCE MANAGEMENT

**Volume 1:** Genes from the Wild
**Volume 2:** Waterlogged Wealth
**Volume 3:** The Threatening Desert
**Volume 4:** Our Common Seas
**Volume 5:** Asking the Earth
**Volume 6:** The Rural Economy and the British Countryside
**Volume 7:** The Water Crisis
**Volume 8:** After the Green Revolution
**Volume 9:** Saving the Seed
**Volume 10:** Unwelcome Harvest
**Volume 11:** The Politics of Industrial Agriculture
**Volume 12:** Forest Politics
**Volume 13:** No Timber Without Trees
**Volume 14:** Controlling Tropical Deforestation
**Volume 15:** Plantation Politics
**Volume 16:** Saving the Tropical Forests
**Volume 17:** Trees, People and Power
**Volume 18:** Tropical Deforestation

# The Politics of Industrial Agriculture

*Tracey Clunies-Ross and Nicholas Hildyard*

publishing for a sustainable future

London • New York

First published in 1992

This edition first published in 2009 by Earthscan

ISBN 978-1-84971-022-0 (Volume 11 hbk)
ISBN 978-1-84971-011-4 (Natural Resource Management set)
ISBN 978-1-84407-930-8 (Earthscan Library Collection)
ISBN 978-0-41585-004-9 (Volume 11 pbk)

For a full list of publications please contact:


Earthscan
2 Park Square, Milton Park, Abingdon, Oxon OX14 4RN
Simultaneously published in the USA and Canada by Earthscan
711 Third Avenue, New York, NY 10017
Earthscan is an imprint of the Taylor & Francis Group, an informa business

First issued in paperback 2013

Earthscan publishes in association with the International Institute for
Environment and Development

A catalogue record for this book is available from the British Library

Library of Congress Cataloging-in-Publication Data has been applied for

**Publisher's note**
The publisher has made every effort to ensure the quality of this reprint, but
points out that some imperfections in the original copies may be apparent.

# The politics of industrial agriculture

Tracey Clunies-Ross and Nicholas Hildyard

EARTHSCAN

Earthscan Publications Ltd, London

First published 1992 by

Earthscan Publications Ltd
120 Pentonville Road, London N1 9JN

**British Library Cataloguing-in-Publication Data**.

A catalogue record for this book is available from the British Library.

ISBN 1-85383-138-7

Typeset by DP Photosetting, Aylesbury, Bucks

Earthscan Publications Ltd is an editorially independent
subsidiary of Kogan Page Ltd and publishes in association with
the International Institute for Environment and Development and
the World Wide Fund for Nature (UK).

# Contents

| | | |
|---|---|---|
| | Acknowledgements | 4 |
| | Introduction | 5 |
| 1 | Industrial Agriculture: Heading for Disaster | 9 |
| 2 | Pushed onto the Treadmill | 40 |
| 3 | Caught on the Treadmill | 59 |
| 4 | The New Barons | 74 |
| 5 | Undermining Alternatives | 83 |
| 6 | Mainstream Responses | 95 |
| 7 | The Real Agenda: GATT and Biotechnology | 105 |
| 8 | Movements for Change | 114 |
| 9 | New Paths | 143 |
| | References | 148 |
| | Index | 163 |

# Acknowledgements

We would like to thank a number of people for help in the discussions and research that preceded this report. In particular, thanks are due to: Tim Lang (Parents for Safe Food), Mark Ritchie (Institute for Agriculture and Trade Policy), Pam Simmons, Simon Fairlie, Larry Lohmann, Patrick McCully (The Ecologist), Richard Hindmarsh (Griffith University), Peter Bane (The Permaculture Activist), George Sobol (Permaculture Association – Britain), Bill Barclay, Meriel Watts, Melanie Miller (Greenpeace), Christine Stevens (Animal Welfare Institute), Michael Fox (The Humane Society of the United States), Isabel Bermejo (CODA/CEPA), Thymio Papayannis (MedWet CoG), Robin Jenkins (Food Commission), Donald Worster (University of Kansas), Mark Purdey (High Barn Farm), Robyn Van En (Indian Line Farm), Christina Groh (Buschberghof), Rosamund Young (Kite's Nest Farm), Pippa Woods (Small Farmers' Association), Jan Juffermans (De Kleine Aarde), David Gibbon (University of East Anglia), Andy Daw (Worcestershire College of Agriculture), Joanne Bower (The Farm and Food Society), Richard Young (Soil Association), Siobhan Mellon, Patrick Holden, Oliver Dowding (British Organic Farmers), Julian Rose (Association of Unpasteurised Milk Producers and Consumers), Alistair Smith (Food Matters), Alan Gear (Henry Doubleday Research Association), John Jearons (Ecology Action of the Midpeninsular), George Porter (Pacific Institute of Resource Management), Arthur Getz, Tony Andersen, George Chan, Robert Waller, David Gordon, Nigel Harle, Sandy Irvine, Harriet Festing, The Men of the Trees (Australia), Members of the SAFE Alliance, together with others, too numerous to mention, who have discussed ideas with us and made suggestions.

We are also grateful to HIVOS for funding the circulation of drafts and to FINNIDA and NOVIB for overall funding of the project. Thanks too to the Goldsmith Foundation for funding our work with the SAFE Alliance.

The opinions in the report are ours alone and do not necessarily reflect the views of SAFE or of the many other organisations which have helped in its preparation.

*Tracey Clunies-Ross and Nicholas Hildyard*

# Introduction

Since the Second World War, agriculture in the Northern industrialised countries has undergone a revolution. Whilst that revolution has dramatically increased yields, it has also been responsible for:

- Extensive rural depopulation and loss of farmers from the land;
- Widespread degradation of the environment;
- Production-related contamination of food with agrochemicals and bacteria;
- An increase in the routine abuse of farm animals; and
- The ruination of Third World economies and livelihoods through the development of unfair trading systems.

Taken separately, the many adverse impacts of industrial agriculture might be held to be mere side effects of an otherwise successful system. Taken together, they paint a picture of a system that is destructive, socially unjust and unsustainable. It is also a system in deep, and growing, crisis.

Confronted by mounting evidence as to the environmental destructiveness of industrial agriculture, and increasingly unable to avoid discussion of its social impacts, mainstream agronomists and policy-makers have belatedly recognized the need for change. "Sustainable agriculture" has become the buzz word of the moment. But "sustainable agriculture" has come to mean all things to all people. The question therefore arises: Sustainable agriculture for whom? Whose interests are we seeking to sustain? And to the detriment of whom?

To answer those questions requires going beyond narrow — and, frankly, sterile — debates on the technologies that might make for a more "sustainable agriculture" and confronting instead the political and economic forces that have driven farmers into agriculture's present disastrous cul-de-sac.

Farmers do not operate in a political or economic vacuum: nor do the retailers and food processors who buy their food and market it to the consumer. The pattern of land ownership, the size of farms and how they

5

are managed; the choice of crops grown, who grows them and how; the role of workers, their pay and conditions; the means by which foodstuffs are processed and marketed, at what cost to their quality and for whose profit; the impact of agriculture on the environment; the prices charged to the consumer; who gains and who loses from the current system; and, ultimately, who enjoys economic and political power are all factors that are shaped not by the decisions of individual farmers or consumers but by the wider political economy in which agriculture operates. The majority of small farmers, for example, have not chosen to leave the land: they have been forced to do so by circumstances over which they have no control.

In that respect, the ability of farmers to make a living is determined not only by the weather and other natural factors, but also by the agricultural policies of their national governments; by the policies of other countries and international agencies; and by international agreements. Neither the formulation of national policies, nor the policies themselves, are "neutral": on the contrary, they reflect the priorities of the dominant interest groups within agriculture and, more broadly, within the food industry as a whole.

It is this set of external influences — and the economic and political structure from which they flow — which has proved the dominant force in shaping the direction that agriculture has taken over the past half century or more. Indeed, governments, international agencies and commercial interests have deliberately manipulated farmers into mechanising production and using "off-farm" chemical inputs to increase output. As production has expanded, prices have been driven down and farmers have been left with little option but to increase production in order to maintain their income. The result is a structurally-encouraged tendency towards overproduction, environmental degradation, and rural depopulation. Increasingly in debt, trapped onto a chemical treadmill, wedded to producing only those crops that bring in the highest return on investment, and vulnerable to even slight changes in prices or in the cost of inputs, many farmers have gone out of business.

Concomitant changes in the food industry — partly the consequence of take-overs, partly the result of new technologies — have compounded the problem by concentrating the control of retailing and processing in fewer and fewer hands. In Britain, 83 per cent of food is now sold through supermarkets, 60 per cent of it being retailed by just five companies.[1] Food distribution has become a centralized operation, and the bulk of food grown in Britain passes through one of just 20 depots. Supermarket chains provide advice to farmers, agree standards to which food is to be grown, often state the amount and timing of chemical applications, grade food, distribute it and retail it. Moreover, by buying in bulk, they have driven down farm gate prices and undermined local and wholesale markets. In the process, producers have become separated from consumers, who now have little control over what they eat or, indeed, the prices they pay for their food; food quality has declined, and, ultimately, public health has been jeopardized.

By favouring some and disadvantaging others, current policies have entrenched the power of specific vested interests and undermined the power of others. The losers have been consumers and smaller producers; the winners, corporations and larger farmers.

Those who have benefitted from the process now dominate policy, pushing the whole process of food production in a direction that serves their immediate and long-term interests. Agricultural research, for example, is dominated by the industry, effectively ensuring that research which supports chemical farming has been funded at the expense of research which would benefit a less-intensive approach. At the farm level, the need to purchase inputs has created a dependency on the agrochemical industry, whose influence on policy has grown correspondingly.

Change to the existing system inevitably threatens those who have most to gain from maintaining the status quo. The influence they currently enjoy on policy has effectively ensured that reform is restricted to those measures that do not undermine their interests. By definition, such measures are generally limited to addressing only the most flagrant abuses of the system and stop far short of the deep structural changes that are needed to achieve a truly sustainable agriculture. In that respect, the strategies now being employed by those who benefit from the system, for retaining their power and control, are among the major factors undermining alternative systems of food production which would liberate farmers from the chemical and financial treadmill on which they find themselves.

At the farm level, such alternatives do not need to be re-invented, merely developed and encouraged. Throughout the industrialised North, there are farmers who, from the outset, have tried to defy conventional wisdom and resist the pressures to adopt intensive chemical farming. Over the years, they have resolutely ploughed their own furrow, developing methods of controlling pests and building fertility which do not rely upon the use of synthetic chemicals. Building upon existing knowledge, individuals have succeeded in creating their own marketing networks, evolving new forms of land ownership, and developing, as far as possible, an agriculture that, in the words of Wendell Berry, "depletes neither soil nor people."[2]

There are no "off-the-shelf", easy blueprints for realizing the promise which the alternatives hold out. On the contrary, differing histories, environments, social conditions and political structures demand a diversity of responses if real change is to be achieved. Groups campaigning in isolation for specific changes in legislation to encourage such alternatives are unlikely to have sufficient influence to challenge the status quo. Problems ranging from environmental degradation to rural depopulation, from dependence on agrochemicals to concentration in the food industry, are interlinked, and cannot be addressed either on a single issue basis or through universal solutions. Indeed, unless groups are aware of the need for a deeper restructuring of industrial society, they may even end up legitimizing the very processes and interests that they are seeking to change.

At issue is the question of power — of who controls the land, inputs, production, marketing, research, decision-making and policy, and with what aims and priorities in mind. In that respect, what unites groups, from farmers to environmentalists, from consumers to animal welfare campaigners, is not an identical vision of the future, but the desire to regain an element of control.

To campaign for changes of a structural nature, it is vital that groups should come together to form alliances which cut across narrow sectoral boundaries, allowing campaigns to be fought on a broader front. In forming such alliances, differences between groups do not magically disappear: the amount of weighting to be given to environmental protection, animal welfare, food quality, price, the protection of local communities, and so on, will always be a matter for negotiation. Those that have begun to form such alliances, however, have come to recognize that though the differences between groups should not be underplayed, they are of less importance than their common commitment to change — and that emphasizing them only plays into the hands of those wielding power.

## Chapter One

# Industrial Agriculture: Heading for Disaster

Since the Second World War, agriculture in the northern industrialised countries has undergone a revolution. Increased mechanisation, the development and widespread use of artificial fertilisers, larger field and farm size, the development of pesticides and herbicides, continuous cropping, increasing farm specialisation, developments in livestock and plant breeding and, now, biotechnology have transformed the landscape and brought major structural changes within the farming community and within rural society.

These changes have brought substantial increases in output, measured most strikingly in terms of output per unit of land. Between 1950 and 1982, yields of wheat in the US rose by 170 per cent, corn by 198 per cent and rice by 296 per cent.[1] Increases of 100 per cent per acre have been recorded for most other major crops.[2] The changes are also reflected in terms of reduced labour input. In Britain, just two per cent of the workforce is now employed in agriculture, and the country has moved from being a net importer of cereals to being the sixth largest exporter in the world.[3] Yields of most basic crops continue to rise by around two per cent a year.

But as the post-war revolution in agriculture has unfolded, so its ruinous impact has become increasingly apparent:

- Hundreds of thousands of farmers and farm workers have been thrown off the land, either because machines and chemicals have made them redundant, or because the high costs of farming have pushed them over the brink into bankruptcy;

- Mechanisation, the use of agrochemicals and the drive to maximise productivity have together caused massive environmental degradation — both at the farm level and beyond;

- Increased output has not brought a healthier, better-fed population; on the contrary, problems of food scarcity have been replaced by the threat of production-related contamination of food with agrochemicals and bacteria;

- Animals have become a mere cog in the food production process: bred for early maturity, crammed together in their thousands, and routinely fed growth promoters and medicaments, their welfare, their health, and the health of those who eat them have been ignored in the quest for cheap food;

- Third World countries have suffered economic ruin and exacerbated famine as their own economies have been sucked into a world trading system which uses their land to provide food for the people and animals of Northern countries, while their farmers have to compete with surpluses dumped on the world market at subsidised prices by the North;

- Meanwhile, the very basis of agriculture is being undermined by the expansion of the wider industrial economy. The energy balance sheet in agriculture is paid little attention, and global warming threatens to render many areas either less productive or completely unproductive.

Taken separately, these adverse impacts of industrial agriculture might be held to be mere side effects of an otherwise successful system; taken together, they paint a picture of a system that is destructive, socially unjust and unsustainable. It is also a system in deep, and growing, crisis.

## Rural Issues and the Land

A first set of concerns relates to the impact of industrial agriculture on the livelihoods of smaller farmers, on the wider economy of rural areas, and on the way people now view their relationship with the land.

## Farmers Leaving the Land

Increasingly chemicals and machinery — both dependent on the use of fossil fuel energy — are used as a substitute for human energy, with the result that large numbers of those formerly employed in agriculture have been driven off the land. Between 1946 and 1989, the total number of people working on farms in Britain (full- and part-time) declined from 976,000 to 285,000.[4] In 1990 alone, 6,000 British farmers sold up, and 4,000 full-time workers lost their jobs.[5]

In the United States, 38 per cent of the workforce was employed in agriculture at the turn of the century, now it is down to three per cent.[6] In the six years between 1980 and 1986, 235,000 farms went out of business, and 650,000 people were lost from the farm workforce. The US Office of Technology Assessment estimates that by the year 2000, the 50,000 largest farms in the US will account for 75 per cent of agricultural production.[7]

Moreover, the capital costs involved in becoming a farmer, mean that opportunities for new entrants are restricted. Increasingly, those entering farming have either inherited their farms, or have built up capital in other ways and switched to farming later in life.

With rising capital costs, spiralling debt has become a hallmark of farming in modern industrial societies. Declining prices in recent years have added to the squeeze on farmers. In the five years between 1984 and 1990, for example, Welsh hill farmers saw their income collapse by 37 per cent in real terms, putting many out of business.[8] It is a pattern that is being repeated in country after country, leading to the increasing concentration of landownership as farms are bought up by larger farmers. The farming community is thus becoming ever more divided between, on the one hand, prosperous "agri-business" farmers who know how to work the system, and, on the other hand, small farmers trying to keep pace with the demands made upon them.[9]

Many areas now support far fewer humans than was common centuries ago.[10] According to Britain's Countryside Commission, the number of upland farmers has contracted due to an increase in the size of farms, which have grown by an average of some 56 per cent in non-afforested areas.[11] The rate at which farms were being amalgamated into larger units more than doubled during the 1960s compared with the previous decade and it continued to increase in the 1970s. In Snowdonia in Wales, 79 per cent of full-time and 70 per cent of part-time workers' jobs disappeared between 1965 and 1972, while on Exmoor and Dartmoor, 66 per cent of full-time jobs were lost between 1952 and 1972.[12] In 1950, less than five per cent of the population lived in the uplands of Britain compared to 20 per cent 200 years before.[13]

## Land as a Commodity

In societies where industrialised agriculture is the norm, land has become little more than one of the factors of production. In Britain, land ownership has traditionally been, and remains, highly inequitable. The top one per cent of the population own 52 per cent of the land, and the top 11 per cent own 92 per cent.[14] In both Britain and the US land has become a commodity which can be freely bought and sold by individuals or corporations, creating a situation in which vast tracts of land are owned by people who are not farmers. In Britain, for example, the Duke of Northumberland owns some 105,000 acres while in Scotland the Duke of Buccleigh owns 277,000 acres, mainly in the southern uplands.[15] In the 1970s and early 1980s, when agriculture was a lucrative investment, large areas of land were also bought by foreign owners, such as the Dutch,[16] and by institutions such as pension funds. The same problem of concentration and control from outside can also be seen in non-agricultural land use. Mining and quarrying in upland areas, for example, is now controlled by big transnational corporations like Rio Tinto Zinc and Consolidated Goldfields.[17] Fish farming on the west coast of Scotland is also often in the hands of wealthy outsiders.

This concept of land as a commodity contrasts strongly with attitudes to land in other cultures. In many parts of Africa, for instance, the concept of owning land was unheard of in the pre-colonial era. Even in Denmark and Norway nobody may buy agricultural land without first obtaining a permit from the Government indicating that he or she has the necessary technical qualifications to farm the land. Moreover, no individual in Denmark may own a farm larger than 180 acres without special permission.[18]

Where there are no controls over land ownership, land becomes an investment or a commodity which must be worked hard to generate

12

short-term profit, often at the expense of the long-term interests of both farmers and the land. When prices are high, there is an incentive to produce as much as possible at the lowest possible price, in order to maximise profits. As prices fall, there is no option but to utilize the land in the most intensive way possible, in order for the business to survive. When prices fall below the level at which they cover the cost of production, land eventually has to be abandoned. Generally, in this system, it is the small farmer who gains least and suffers first.

When agricultural returns are poor, as at the present time, land as a commodity becomes worth less and less. In Britain, with the close link between agricultural returns and land prices, collapsing farm incomes have led to the near halving of land prices in under a decade, leaving over-borrowed farmers facing bankruptcy. In Australia, where there is even less protection from the vagaries of the world market, farmers are unable to sell up and leave farming as no one will buy their farms. To build sustainable farming practices when teetering on the knife-edge between profitability and bankruptcy is next to impossible.

## Women in Farming

Division of tasks between men and women on farms has been a feature of rural life through the centuries, and throughout the world. With the development of industrial farming, there has been a tendency for the division of tasks to degenerate into a conceptual division between conscious, productive tasks (men's work) and "natural", unproductive and unskilled tasks (women's work). Detailed studies of women's duties on farms in the US show that women regularly undertake household and childcare responsibility, 74 per cent also grow vegetables and rear animals for family consumption, 61 per cent undertake bookkeeping and other secretarial duties for the business, while 47 per cent run farm errands, and 37 per cent take care of farm animals.[19]

As farms have become increasingly linked to the wider market economy, the conditions of women's participation in farming has changed. Often their tasks in the formal production sphere have been made more casual, and they have lost self-determination over production and activities. There is also a tendency for fewer farm activities to be solely their responsibility.[20] Nevertheless, the productivity of farms, particularly family farms, is

13

directly related to the free availability of a houseworker and "another pair of hands" for farm labour.

The general recasting of women's roles in agriculture as mere "supporters" of the "producers" has led to the further misconception that women have disappeared from agriculture. In common parlance, farmers are now men, and women are connected with them in some way, for instance as "farmers' wives". By talking of "a farmer and his family", the contribution made by women and children to farming has been made invisible by story-tellers, researchers, economists and planners. Yet, despite this myth, the 1981 British population census revealed that 25,430 women were farmers, farm-managers or horticulturalists (11 per cent of the total). There were also 26,600 women farm workers (17 per cent) and 8,140 women horticultural workers (44 per cent of the total). Furthermore, a detailed study of the role of women in British farms showed that 70 per cent of them were involved in some way in manual work on the farm, 32 per cent on a regular basis.[21]

Despite the persistence of women's contribution to farming, the need for them to "disappear'" remains compelling. In industrial agricultural systems, sons rather than daughters or wives usually inherit the farm, with women, rather than men, marrying into farming families. It is also interesting to note that, in the UK until 1976, the occupier of an agricultural holding completing the labour section of the annual census form was instructed to "exclude the wives of farmers, partners and directors, even though the wives themselves may be partners or directors."[22]

## Compartmentalized Thinking about Land

The recasting of women's relationships with the land, and with men, is part of a wider change in the relationship between people and the land in industrial society. In the industrialised countries of the North, where the majority of the population was urbanized generations ago, the perception of agriculture and the natural environment has changed, with different aspects of the relationship between humans and the land becoming compartmentalized. As a result, public policy is often driven by conflicting demands. On the one hand, consumer organisations call for "efficient" agriculture that produces low cost, sanitised food, while, on the other, consumers — seduced by advertisements for food which portray farms as unchanging idyllic places, where animals roam freely and the pace of life is slow — appear unaware of the implications of "efficiency" for animal welfare and the environment.

On the one hand, land is nothing more than a factor of production, and is the responsibility of farmers, who may use whatever techniques they think appropriate to produce food "efficiently" (*see* Box below). On the other hand, land as an amenity, land for its scenic beauty, land as part of the "rural idyll", land as a reserve for rare plants and animals, and land as part of the natural environment continues to be the subject of great public concern.

Having lost their connection with the land and with farmers, urban-based populations often seem unable to see the problem as a whole. Shocked by the reality of intensive animal production or environmental destruction, large sections of the public join pressure groups to demand change (one in ten British people belong to an environmental group), whilst as consumers and taxpayers they continue to support policies and approaches which result in intensive farming, rural dislocation and environmental damage.

---

## The Myth of Efficiency

Efficiency is a term that is readily used and rarely defined. Questions are beginning to be asked about the meaning of "sustainable" agriculture, but the use of the term "efficient" is hardly ever questioned. Efficient agricultural systems, certainly in the British and European context, are thought to be ones that produce food at the lowest cost. Yet an acceptance that the term efficient relates solely to the economic context creates a number of serious problems.

In economic terms, for any given situation, at a single point in time, there will be one crop which gives better returns than any other. The logical outcome of a demand for efficient agriculture is therefore specialisation and monocultures. Monocultures require large inputs of non-renewable energy to provide fertilisers and chemical pest and weed control. There is also an inevitable tendency for farms in the same area to concentrate on the same crop, which means that the crops have to be transported out of the area to be traded for other monoculturally grown crops from other areas. Dependence on

---

non-renewable inputs, transport, and sophisticated marketing thus become almost inevitable consequences of economically efficient agriculture.

Furthermore, agricultural systems are clearly at their most efficient, in terms of reducing the unit cost of production, when they treat health and the environment as "externalities". Vast cereal monocultures, for instance, which use artificial fertilisers to provide fertility, pesticides to control crop losses, and large machinery to reduce labour, provide grain at a low unit cost. In this calculation, loss of wildlife and their habitats, soil erosion, contamination of water, pesticide residues in food, and the destruction of rural communities do not have a cost. Consumers pay less for their food, but as taxpayers or consumers they have to pay to remove pesticides and nitrates from the water; as environmentalists, they donate money to campaigns to stamp out the practices which provide their cheap food.

The logical outcome of demanding food at the lowest possible unit cost is not just the degradation of the environment and the possible contamination of food and water with agrochemicals. If unit costs must be reduced, then inputs such as labour, which are expensive, must also be reduced. This can be achieved by shedding labour, for instance by crowding animals together in intensive rearing systems which can be largely automated. It can also be achieved by driving down rates of pay for agricultural labour, or by employing casual workers instead of permanent ones.

Conventional wisdom would have us believe that big units are more efficient than small ones. On very small units, if the labour input is fairly costed, unit costs do tend to be higher. Set against this, however, land worked with intensive labour input (for example, organic horticultural holdings), as opposed to intensive fossil fuel input, often make very efficient use of natural resources, whilst also producing a high output.

In the case of small- and medium-sized farms, versus big farms, the economics of production have become hopelessly skewed by subsidies. In economic theory, farmers produce for a market, and compete with each other to supply that market: the most efficient thrive. In Europe and in the US, taxpayer subsidies are linked to the volume of output: the biggest and most intensive farmers pick up the lion's share of the subsidies, and they thrive. This should not be interpreted as economic efficiency. In fact, in the current situation, where the EC for instance overproduces grain, the larger the volume of grain a farm produces, the more it costs the EC in storage and export subsidies. Taken to its logical absurdity (which it now has been) it becomes cheaper to pay farmers to produce nothing (set-aside) than to buy their grain. Within this economic framework, small, less-intensive farmers should be seen as being more efficient as they produce fewer unwanted surpluses.

In effect, it is almost impossible to tell who is producing most efficiently. Past subsidies for fuel, for drainage, for irrigation, for research into high input/high output agriculture, not to mention current subsidies, produce a completely distorted picture. All that can be said with any certainty is that current policies continue to favour large, intensive farmers.

Economies of scale are often thought to relate solely to the efficient use of resources, but they can also be related to power. Small farmers buying anything from seeds and fertilisers, to large agricultural machinery are likely to pay more than big farmers, because they have less bargaining power in the market place. Individuals and small businesses also have to pay higher rates of interest on borrowed money, as well as higher charges on transactions. However inefficient they are at using their resources to produce food, big farms always have a head start in terms of lower input costs. Very big farms have considerably greater power to negotiate favourable terms for their inputs, which means that even if they are less efficient at turning those inputs into output they can still survive, but if they operate at a reasonable level of efficiency they can undercut the smaller producers, squeezing competitors out of business and further enhancing their own power.

In the food industry, corporate clout is now taking over from efficiency as the reason why larger businesses are increasing their market share. Big companies are able to reduce the costs of production and drive out competitors not just by introducing new technology and increasing efficiency, but by using their enormous buying power to force farmers to accept less for their products, and by cutting wage rates in the production industry, effectively forcing other firms to do the same or go under. Once a few big firms have come to dominate a sector, it is their power to manipulate the market, rather than their efficiency, which prevents serious challengers from emerging.

The compartmentalized approach which has developed in industrial societies, also leads to the belief that different land uses necessarily compete. Land is therefore designated for a certain use: it is seen as being for building, for wildlife, for growing food, for forestry, or for recreation. The old interactions between these activities is effectively disappearing.

## Rural Dislocation

With the decline in the number of farms, and farmers, has come a decline in rural services and an increase in rural deprivation. Though depopulation *per se* is levelling off in many parts of Britain, the age structure of local communities is increasingly skewed towards older inhabitants. Indeed a vicious cycle seems to be at work in which the number of school children falls, schools are shut, people with young families move out and shops, bus services and other facilities decline through lack of support. At the same time, the cost of goods on sale in local shops tends to be considerably higher than in the cities (even for produce that is grown or reared locally). In many areas, the housing stock is not only poor and limited but also vulnerable to 'gentrification' as urban commuters and second homers look for rural retreats.[23] In Gwynedd in Wales in the early 1980s, for example, there were twice as many holiday homes as there were families on the council waiting list.[24] The focus on 'growth centres', particularly in the Scottish Highlands, seems to have aggravated the drift of people away from more remote areas, albeit to a closer destination. Cultural diversity is also undermined by the import of more homogenous lifestyles and values.[25]

In parts of Southern Europe, such as Spain, the process of abandoning small scale, local infrastructures for education, health and so on, is also operating in parallel with the process of industrialising agriculture. Here, it is not necessarily the decline in the number of farmers that has precipitated the decline in rural services. Where the economic and political interests of those with power are served by the development of macro-infrastructural developments, many services are removed from the rural areas. The Spanish reform of education, for instance, has led to the closing of many rural schools, as children over 11 years old are sent to large, distant, "modern" education centres. In these areas the industrialisation of agriculture is merely one part of the wider industrial approach to reshaping rural society.[26]

## *Threats to Health*

The industrialisation of agriculture also poses a direct threat to the health of farm workers and those living in the countryside. In Britain, for example, it is estimated that some 2,500 farmers have been permanently affected by the use of organo-phosphorous compounds in sheep dips,[27] and by 1992 the National Farmers Union itself was worried enough about the situation to be carrying out its own investigation. In 1984, when Friends of the Earth first started a pesticides campaign in Britain, hundreds of cases of pesticide poisoning were uncovered. The incidents occurred mainly as a result of spray drift and involved children and others walking on footpaths, as well as farmers and farm workers.[28] In 1987, evidence given to the House of Lords Select Committee into pesticides and human health revealed that the 4,000 cases of acute pesticide poisoning registered each year with the NHS National Poisons Unit seriously under-estimated the true scale of the problem.[29]

# Environmental Degradation and Industrial Agriculture

A second set of concerns relates to the environmental impact of industrialised agriculture, which in many areas has been little short of devastating.

## *Loss of Wildlife and Wildlife Habitats*

As farmers have brought more and more land into production, the loss of wildlife habitats has been severe.

In Britain alone, 621,000 kilometres of hedgerow — or 22 per cent of the total — was lost between 1947 and 1985.[30] Hedges provide homes for mammals, birds and reptiles, cover for a range of herbaceous plants and small trees, and an important windbreak to stop soil erosion. A traditional mixed hedge also supplies fruit and other food for birds, mammals and insects. Recent research carried out by the University of Southampton and The Game Conservancy Trust under contract from the Ministry of Agriculture, Fisheries and Food (MAFF) suggests that large field sizes create particular problems for pest control. These bodies are now advocating the breaking up of large fields with "ridges" which, like hedge banks, provide the right conditions for predatory insects and spiders to overwinter, so that in the spring they can move out into the crop, reducing pest numbers significantly. The benefits of encouraging natural predators are now recognized to be so significant (even in purely financial terms) that it is thought to be cost-efficient to reintroduce "ridges" to break up large fields.[31]

Just as the upward pressure on farm size and the need to use bigger, more "efficient" machinery has led to the removal of hedgerows, so the adoption of industrial methods of production has had a dramatic effect on the survival of wildlife habitats. As farmers have had to increase production from their land, they have used fertilisers, herbicides and drainage to "improve" their grassland; they have selected a few useful plant varieties and eliminated the rest. This has been severely detrimental for wildlife, with bees, butterflies and insects no longer able to thrive on this type of farmland. Changing management techniques, such as the switch from hay to silage making, also mean that the first cut is taken much earlier in the year, thus disturbing wildlife, particularly ground-nesting birds, and preventing the reproduction of wildflowers.[32]

In many upland areas of Britain, stocking densities increased between 1955 and 1976 by 80 per cent.[33] Intensive grazing undermines the ability of moorland vegetation to stabilise itself, thus triggering a downward spiral of vegetation and soils, leading to soil erosion. The impact of unrestricted grazing is amplified in some areas by burning to create more suitable ground cover not just for sheep, but also grouse and deer. Large scale and/ or repeated burning can have the effect of reducing the supply of soil nutrients, such as phosphorous, encouraging soil erosion and increasing the sediment in local streams and rivers.[34]

In lowland areas, old, unimproved (species-rich) meadows are an important habitat for many plants and insects. In the last 40 years, 97 per cent of Britain's species-rich meadows have been destroyed, and 80 per cent of sheep-grazed chalk and limestone grassland has gone.[35] Despite the fact that land is considered to be in "surplus", the destruction continues. For example, half of England's wildlife-rich limestone grassland is in Gloucestershire, where 40 per cent of sites were damaged between 1978 and 1987. In Devon, 65 per cent of the unprotected wet, heathy grasslands of the Culm Meadows were destroyed in only five years. The Royal Society for Nature Conservation has launched an appeal to save the Meadows, arguing that "unless urgent action is taken, the only meadows that will survive into the next century will be those that receive special protection as nature reserves, Sites of Special Scientific Interest (SSSIs), or Areas of Special Scientific Interest (ASSIs)".[36]

Changes in farming practices have thus had a dramatic effect on wildlife. Out of the 55 species of butterfly which breed in Britain, one (the Large Blue butterfly) became extinct in 1979, 8 more species are endangered, and another 12 have declined so much that they are now officially rare. Out of 43 species of dragonfly, 3 have become extinct, 12 are endangered, rare or vulnerable. But the list does not stop there. In 1988, the Department of the Environment listed 1,685 insects, 149 plants, 51 breeding birds and 25 mammals breeding on land as endangered, rare or vulnerable.[37]

Problems of wildlife and habitat loss are acute in Britain, both because such a large proportion of the land in Britain is "farmed" — and it is therefore important that farming and wildlife should be able to co-exist — and because Britain has gone so far down the road of "agricultural efficiency". Over the centuries, farming practices have helped to shape the landscape, and different forms of wildlife have developed particular niches within that landscape. It is therefore not farming *per se* which threatens wildlife, but the adoption of industrialised farming techniques.

However, Britain is by no means unique in this respect. As intensive agricultural practices are increasingly being forced on Southern Europe, wildlife habitats are being destroyed. More than 40 per cent of Europe's wildlife habitats are located in Southern Europe, and road building, dams, land amalgamation, forestry plantations, the use of big machinery and agro-chemicals, all attracting EC financial support, are having a devastating impact (*see* p.49).

In Southern Spain, for example, one of the most important areas of wetland in Europe — the Donana National Park — is threatened by intensive agriculture in the surrounding area. Changes in agricultural practice have led to a fall in the water table, through aquifer over-exploitation, and to water pollution by fertilisers and pesticides. The result has been the death of thousands of breeding waterfowl every year, and the endangering of the last winter refuge of many thousands of geese and other Northern European birds. Other sites, such as Daimiel, a Ramsar wetland site in Castilla La Mancha, has almost dried up in recent years due to over-exploitation of the aquifer to irrigate surrounding farmland. Throughout Europe many wetlands have been drained for cultivation. The threat to wetlands in Europe is so profound that the Mediterranean Wetland (MedWet) Forum has been set up to try and halt and reverse the loss of Mediterranean wetlands. This issue has brought together participants from Mediterranean EC member governments, the Ramsar and Barcelona Convention secretariats, the EC Commission (DGXI), a number of prominent organisations in the field (IUCN, ICBP, IWRB, WWF, RSPB, Tour du Valat, Greek Wetland Centre) and various experts.[38]

Outside Europe, in North America, wetlands and other natural habitats are equally threatened by industrialised agriculture. In the US, more than 870,000 km$^2$ of wetlands (more than half the original total) have been lost, 87 per cent of them being converted to farmland or rangelands.[39] Birds such as cranes which depend almost entirely on wetlands for their survival have become severely endangered. The whooping crane of North America hovers on the brink of extinction, while other species, including the Siberian and Japanese cranes, are almost as rare.[40]

Rangelands, which once covered the vast expanse of the North American Great Plains and supported 60 million bison, have also been converted into farmland on a massive scale. Rangelands may look uniform from a distance, but can contain up to 80 different species of grass, together with many other small plants, and, when not overgrazed and degraded, can provide food for large numbers of wild animals as well as livestock. When such rangelands are ploughed and planted with vast cereal monocultures, they lose their diversity and consequently their value as wildlife habitats.[41]

## Soil Erosion

The impact of industrial agriculture on the land itself has also been severe. With its artificial fertilisers and chemical sprays, modern chemical farming has disastrously undermined the natural fertility of soils. As farmers have ceased to apply manure and other organic material to the land — instead spreading artificial fertiliser by the trailer-load — so the soil's structure in many areas has begun to break down, increasing its vulnerability to erosion.

Every year, some 24 billion tonnes of soil are eroded from the world's agricultural lands, enough soil to fill a train of freight cars stretching from the Earth to the moon — and back again five times.[42] In the UK, erosion has increased significantly over the past 30 years. A prime cause has been the three-fold expansion of land under winter cereals, which leaves the land unprotected by vegetation during the wettest parts of the year. Official figures suggest an annual rate of soil loss of about two and a half tonnes per hectare: a recent report by the Soil Association, however, revealed that some fields were losing as much as 40 tonnes per hectare in a single year.[43] Other studies have shown that whilst average losses from some soils might be 15 to 17 tonnes per hectare per year, in bad years this could go up to over 400 tonnes per hectare.[44] In the US, where erosion has long been acknowledged a problem, losses of 30 tonnes an acre are not uncommon.[45] In fact, it is estimated that one third of the top-soil base in the US has been lost over the last 200 years.[46] In the early 1980s, the US as a whole saw one billion tonnes of soil washed or blown away from its 290 million acres of cultivated land. In terms of lost productivity, this is equivalent to losing over 400,000 hectares of agricultural land a year.[47]

## Soil Compaction

The introduction of heavy farm machinery has compounded the problem of soil degradation. With modern ploughing methods, a tractor can pass over the same land six or seven times. The soil becomes compacted, reducing its ability to absorb water, which runs-off the soil and therefore increases erosion. Hard layers or "lenses" of compacted soil are formed well below the soil surface. These can impede the growth of plant roots, the flow of air, the transport of nutrients and the flow of moisture in the soil.[48]

Yields can be significantly reduced by such compaction. A study of maize and soya bean cultivation in Minnesota concluded that soil compaction was the worst problem faced by modern farmers in that area. During wet years when compaction was most severe, maize yields fell by 7.5 per cent, sugar beet yields by 13 per cent and potato yields by half. In the US as a whole, soil compaction is estimated to have cost farmers $3 billion in 1980 due to lost yields.[49]

## Salinization and Waterlogging

In arid areas, such as the south-western United States and parts of the

Mediterranean and the USSR, the introduction of perennial irrigation has brought the added problem of salinization. Irrigation agriculture is one of the most productive forms of farming. In the US, a Nebraska corn farmer can produce 40 bushels of corn a year on one acre of unirrigated land. By introducing irrigation, that yield can be trebled.[50] But year after year irrigation on poorly drained land has waterlogged the soils in many irrigated areas, causing salts in the groundwater to rise to the surface, where they accumulate, turning vast stretches of farmland into salt-encrusted desert.

In many areas, irrigated land is now so severely degraded that it is unfit for agriculture. According to the US Salinity Laboratory, 25 to 35 per cent of all irrigated land in the country suffers from salinity problems.[51]

## Toxic Pollutants

The health and productivity of agricultural land is also threatened by pollution, partly as a result of the use of agrochemicals and partly due to pollution from non-agricultural sources. For years, it was denied that pesticides could contaminate the soil for more than a brief period, since it was assumed that they would either break down or become bound to soil particles and thus immobilized. But many pesticides have now been found to persist in the soil for far longer than previously thought possible. A case in point is the carcinogenic pesticide Ethylene Dibromide (EDB), now banned in several countries, which can survive in the soil for more than 20 years. Its persistence results from traces of the pesticide becoming locked away in the soil's micropores, where they are out of reach of the micro-organisms that would normally degrade them.[52] Numerous toxic chemicals, including PCBs and many industrial solvents, behave similarly in the soil. Should the soil be disturbed, however, they can be released to re-enter the environment. The implications for the future contamination both of agricultural lands and underlying groundwaters are horrendous.

In the south-west of Holland, air pollution from factories along the Belgium–Netherlands border has caused such extensive contamination of the soil that local residents have been advised not to grow vegetables.[53] The dumping of toxic wastes on land has also contaminated thousands of hectares throughout Europe and the US.

In Czechoslovakia, 150 tonnes of cadmium are added to the soil each year from industrial emissions; an equivalent amount being added through the use of phosphate fertilisers containing 100 parts per million (ppm) of cadmium.

Environmental pollution is thought to be one of the principal reasons for poor life expectancy in Czechoslovakia. As Tomas Zidek, from the Czechoslovakian Agricultural Ministry has pointed out, "Consumers can change their habits by eating less fat and sugar, and by stopping smoking, but they can do little about the contamination of their food."[54]

## Groundwater Depletion

Rising demand for water for irrigated agriculture has led to the massive overexploitation of groundwaters in many parts of the industrialised world. As a result, wells are drying up and irrigated land is being forced out of production.

In the USA, one-fifth of all irrigated land is watered by groundwater extracted from the Ogallala aquifer, a body of water equal to that in Lake Huron. It took nearly half a million years for that groundwater to accumulate: at current rates of extraction, however, it will be depleted within 25–50 years. Since the 1940s, 500 cubic kilometres of water have been withdrawn from the aquifer, almost all of it for agriculture. Such is the rate at which it is being depleted that some areas have already run out of water. In Texas alone, over 2,000 square kilometres of irrigated land have been withdrawn from production and a further 7,800 square kilometres are expected to be without water within the decade.[55] All told, almost half of the irrigated land in the US is in areas where groundwater tables are declining by more than one foot a year. Unless farmers reduce pumping, some four million hectares will eventually have to be withdrawn from irrigated agriculture.[56]

Calls by environmentalists to limit the abstraction of groundwater have fallen on deaf ears. In the San Joaquin Valley of California, one of the major areas of irrigated farming in the United States, the rate of groundwater pumping now exceeds replenishment by more than half a trillion gallons a year — and by the end of the century that figure is expected to double. Much of the land is farmed by large corporations — Exxon, Getty Oil and Texaco to name but a few — and their lobbying has ensured that virtually no controls exist over the amount of groundwater they are allowed to extract.[57]

In the southwest, those states dependent on the Ogallala aquifer have taken a deliberate policy decision to continue present rates of extraction, insisting that groundwater left in the ground is water wasted. The prospect of the Ogallala running dry does not disturb them: by then, they argue, alternative water supplies will be available as a result of river diversion schemes. Such diversion schemes will cause massive ecological damage, however, and are also likely to prove too expensive to build. The chances are that, sooner or later, the arid southwest of the USA will simply run out of water.

## Ground and Surface Water Pollution

The intensive use of land is also contributing to the contamination of water resources. In the USA, some 50 million Americans are potentially at risk from pesticide contaminated groundwaters, a problem that now affects 26 states in the union.[58] Two of the most pervasive of the pesticides, Alachlor and Atrazine, are known to cause cancer in laboratory animals, and are probable human carcinogens.[59] In Iowa, more than a quarter of the state's drinking water is contaminated.[60] In Poverty Bay, in New Zealand, Atrazine levels of 37 parts per billion were found in groundwater — 370 times EC permissible levels for pesticide residues in drinking water.[61] In Britain, pesticide contamination of water is also a major problem, a 1991 report by Friends of the Earth revealing that some ten million consumers in England, mainly in the south and east, regularly receive water contamined with levels of pesticides above EC safety limits.[62]

Nitrates, which in large doses can cause "blue baby syndrome", and which are suspected of causing stomach cancer, are also a major contaminant in many groundwaters. The major source of nitrates are artificial fertilisers, the use of which has doubled worldwide over the past 20 years. Farmyard manure from feedlots is also a source of nitrate pollution. In Britain, where one-third of water supplies are drawn from groundwaters, 7 per cent of wells consistently exceed the EC safety limit of 50 milligrams per litre, jeopardizing the water supplies of 1.8 million people. Moreover, nitrate levels in groundwater are steadily increasing, the number of public drinking water wells which exceeded the limit more than doubling between 1970 and 1987.[63] Concern has reached such a level that the British

Government has now introduced an experimental scheme of Nitrate Sensitive Areas, in which certain farming activities are restricted or prohibited. In the Brie area of France, nitrate levels in the Petite Traconne spring, one of the many sources supplying Paris with its drinking water, have trebled over the past 30 years and regularly exceed official safety limits.[64]

## Food Quality and the Consumer

A third set of concerns relates to the safety and quality of the food which is produced and processed using industrial methods of agriculture and food production.

There is no doubt that in countries like Britain, the post-war food revolution has brought an end to the problems of food scarcity and has given consumers access to an increased range of foods, including those associated with other countries and cultures. Expenditure on food as a percentage of the household budget has also declined. But, as the former Director of the London Food Commission (now Director of Parents for Safe Food), Tim Lang, has pointed out, there has been "a jump out of the frying pan of scarcity into the fire of environmental and public health problems which are avoidable".[65]

### Processed Foods

Processed foods now make up the major part of the diet of those in industrialised countries. Because of the huge buying power of food manufacturers, their ability to dictate prices to farmers, and their vast economies of scale, processed foods have become cheap. Processed foods are also easier to transport and store than fresh fruit and vegetables, and are designed to be easier to prepare and cook. There is therefore an inbuilt price incentive to purchase processed food.

But food produced and processed by industrialised methods is not always what it seems. From just a few basic ingredients — primary products such as cotton seed, corn, soybean and fishmeal — modern "food technologists" are able to manufacture "foods" that look and taste like beef, mutton or cheese but which have nothing in common with the natural product.[66] Food processing almost inevitably reduces the "biological sophistication" of food, with processed foods containing only a minute fraction of the chemicals present in natural foods.[67] Synthetic orange juice, such as that sold in children's sugary drinks, may consist of just 10 chemicals, while a real orange has many hundreds. Those with an interest in public ill-health — from doctors to food campaigners — have consistently identified processed foods as an area of concern.

## Additives

In Britain, almost three-quarters of the food consumed is processed.[68] The use of additives — chemicals added deliberately to the food in the course of processing — rose ten-fold between 1955 and 1985, by which time the average Briton was eating 8–10 lbs of additives a year.[69] Some 4,000 additives are commonly used in food, around 93 per cent of them for purely cosmetic purposes, their function being to modify the taste, appearance, and texture of food. Processing aids, preservatives, anti-oxidants and sequestrants make up the other 7 per cent.[70]

The use of additives is defended by industry and government on the grounds that they can be used to reduce the incidence of bacterial food poisoning, lengthen shelf lives, and make food more attractive and cheaper. But, as the use of additives has grown, so have concerns over their health effects and questions as to their need. The sensitivity of individuals to chemicals in general, and additives in particular, varies enormously and, even in small doses, some additives can cause adverse reactions. A number of additives are proven or suspected animal carcinogens, teratogens or both.

## Regulation

The majority of additives are unregulated and few have been tested for their full range of health effects. In Britain, for example, only 10 per cent of the additives in use are regulated by the EC. Yet, in 1987, an independent watchdog agency, the London Food Commission, estimated that 70 per cent of food preservatives, 50 per cent of anti-oxidants and 50 per cent of food colourants currently in use are known or suspected hazards.[71] Even where controls do exist, they differ widely from country to country. Of the 17 artificial colours permitted for use in Britain, 10 are banned in the USA and all are banned in Norway.

In theory, consumers can avoid additives by buying food that does not contain them. But the labelling on products is often confusing and tells consumers little or nothing about the safety of the additives listed. In the UK, for example, a product labelled "strawberry-flavoured" must contain strawberry, but a product labelled "strawberry flavour" need contain no strawberry, the flavour coming entirely from additives. Harmonization of EC standards by 1993 will rationalize food labelling throughout Europe, but this will only enshrine the use of additives and does not tackle the critical issue of whether they are needed in the first place. Essentially, the "need" for additives boils down to a commercial requirement to make "long shelf-life" food look like real food.

The centralization of food processing and distribution has taken control over what goes into their food out of the hands of consumers. Consumer protection has therefore become dependent on regulations. Yet food safety regulations are presided over by governments and international bodies which are heavily influenced by industry. The decisions which are taken clearly reflect a compromise between industry and public health concerns: some bodies and governments responding more to public health concerns than others. There is also concern that "deregulation" is undermining existing food standards. Although consumers with fears about food safety can boycott certain foods, the absence of direct links between producers and consumers means that farmers producing safe food are penalized by general scares, and farmers producing contaminated food are protected by their anonymity.

## Pesticides in Food

Even if consumers take care to avoid particular additives, they may not be able to avoid chemicals added unintentionally to their food — either through pollution or as a result of modern farming techniques. Most crops are now routinely sprayed several times with pesticides before harvesting, and often several times more after harvesting. By the early 1980s, 97–98 per cent of all main crops, cereals and vegetables in Britain were sprayed at least once.[72]

Like additives, the testing of the effects of pesticides on health, though very costly, leaves a lot to be desired, and much of it is out of date. In the early 1980s, some 45,000 different pesticide products were on the market in the

US, formulated from 1,400 active ingredients.[73] Of those active ingredients, 600 were in common use. Yet, according to the US National Academy of Sciences, only 37 per cent had been adequately tested. Information on the health effects of the rest was "insufficient" to complete a full assessment of their health hazards. There was no safety data at all for 37 per cent of the active ingredients in common use.[74] Although the US Environmental Protection Agency has undertaken to review the safety data on pesticides, it does not foresee the review being completed before the turn of the century and many new pesticides are still being introduced onto the market before the full range of required tests have been carried out.[75]

Where information does exist on the health effects of pesticides, it is far from reassuring. A 1985 report by the London Food Commission found that 49 pesticides in common use in the UK were possible carcinogens, 61 were suspected mutagens and 90 possible alergens. Thirty-nine of the pesticides were banned for use in other countries.[76] In the US, the National Research Council estimated that 30 per cent of insecticides, 60 per cent of herbicides and 90 per cent of fungicides could cause tumours. It has been calculated that one in 200 cases of cancer in America are caused by pesticides, although that figure is thought by many to be an underestimate.[77]

Much of our food routinely — and lawfully — contains residues of these pesticides. In 1989, Britain's Ministry of Agriculture, Fisheries and Food (MAFF) released the results of a nationwide survey of pesticide residues in food. The Ministry was forced to admit that "there is no such thing as a pesticide-free food in Britain".[78] The report revealed that food was still contaminated with DDT, despite a ban on its use; that babies are likely to exceed the World Health Organization's Acceptable Daily Intake levels for organochlorines if they drink baby milk prepared from cow's milk; that the residue levels of many pesticides exceed official Maximum Residue Limits (MRLs); that 58 per cent of infant rusks sampled contained organophosphate pesticides; and that 67 per cent of white bread samples were contaminated with pesticides.[79] Many known carcinogens were among the residues reported, including lindane, dieldrin, pentachlorophenol, malathion, captan, parathion and others.

Even where a pesticide has been banned for use, Northern consumers may still be exposed to residues in imported food. Many banned pesticides are exported for use in the Third World and return as residues on imported food. Although tests on imported foods are limited, they frequently reveal high levels of pesticide residues. In Britain, the pesticide lindane — banned in Germany, the Netherlands and Japan and severely restricted in 16 other countries (although still permitted in Britain) — has been found in cocoa imported from Brazil, albeit in minute quantities. Imports of pork and chicken from China are similarly contaminated.[80] US Food and Drug Administration figures have revealed that 10 per cent of food imported into the US contains illegal levels of detectable pesticides.[81]

A frequent excuse for inaction over pesticide residues in food has been the claim that residues are present at such low levels that they are unlikely to be harmful. However, as Peter Snell of the London Food Commission pointed out: "There is a substantial body of medical opinion which believes that since cancer is caused at the level of the individual cell, there is no safe level for a carcinogen".[82]

# Animals as Conversion Machines

A fourth set of concerns relates to the use of animals as part of a process to convert raw materials into higher value products, without any concern for the welfare of the animals or those who eventually consume them.

## Battery Farms

The treadmill in agriculture does not relate solely to the use of chemicals in the field: animal production has also got caught on the "merry-go-round to hell".[83] Consumers want cheaper animal products and farmers want to make a profit; increasingly, therefore, capital has been substituted for labour. To maximise production and minimise labour costs, farmers have turned towards intensive methods of livestock rearing. Gone are the days when chickens were free to wander around the farmyard at will, or when calves were reared with their mothers: today, they are crammed into cages, fed hormones to boost their growth and antibiotics to stave off the diseases that come with overcrowding.

In Britain alone, 50 million egg-laying battery hens are crowded into small cages where standing up and stretching the neck can be difficult, and spreading of the wings is absolutely impossible.[84] Broiler chickens are raised in huge sheds containing 5,000 to 100,000 birds, where for the whole of their seven-week lives they do little but stand and peck at the food that passes by on a conveyor belt, or at their neighbours. Thanks to genetic and nutritional "progress" they now reach the same weight in 42 days that they used to reach in 84 days.[85] Their bodies become too heavy for their legs and they sink down into the ammonia-ridden litter, developing burns and deformities. One in 20 die before they reach slaughter weight.[86] Calves destined for the veal market, and pigs, are kept in similarly cramped conditions, unable to turn round, or even to move backwards and forwards.

These kinds of animal rearing systems have developed as a result of efforts to lower the unit cost of production. But animals are not machines, and even people unconcerned about animal welfare issues acknowledge that battery food production brings its own problems. Fed on a diet of fish, bones, feathers, dried blood, offal and even "human effluent", the animals raised in today's battery units are often severely infected with bacteria such as salmonella. In Britain, the incidence of salmonella has now reached epidemic proportions — cases of salmonella infection rising 12-fold between 1982 and 1988.[87] In the USA, salmonella is rife in egg and egg-based products. To combat salmonella and other infections, farmers have dosed animal feeds with antibiotics. As a result of their widespread and indiscriminate use, more than eight antibiotics used for treating humans are now ineffective due to bacteria acquiring resistance to them.[88]

Hormones, used to accelerate the growth process in animals, are also problematic. Several growth hormones have now been banned in the EC and North America as carcinogens but there is strong evidence that the illicit use of banned hormones still thrives. The consumption of hormone residues in meat has been linked to premature breast development amongst young girls and to other signs of precocious sexual development, studies in Puerto Rico reporting cases of children as young as three years old developing pubic hair.[89]

Factory farming is not just bad for animals and the humans that eat them, but also for the humans who work in the production system. In the US, descriptions of the conditions in chicken slaughterhouses, given as testimony on a bill introduced by Senator Howard Metzenbaum, left little room for doubt about the problems involved.[90] Quite apart from the inhumane conditions imposed on the birds, the workers employed in chicken slaughterhouses often suffer repetitive motion injuries, such as carpal tunnel syndrome and tendonitis. Moreover the scale of such problems is growing. In 1989, the Empire Kosher Foods poultry plant in Pennsylvania was fined $1.36 million by the Occupational Safety and Health Administration for "knowingly and willfully" exposing workers to cumulative trauma injuries. In the same year a plant owned by Cargill was fined $242,000 and also cited for "knowingly and willfully" injuring about half of its workers.[91] The problem is made worse by the growing concentration in the poultry industry which means that the scale of operations is continually increasing. In the US, four companies now produce 41 per cent of all poultry, 20 companies produce 79 per cent.[92]

## Genetic Engineering

With the advent of genetic engineering, a new generation of potential food problems has come into play. In Britain, genetically-engineered strains of yeast have now been approved for use in bread-making, and rennet in cheese, although the consumer will not know what products they have been used in. Their long-term health effects are largely unknown.

Controversy already surrounds the use of Bovine Somatotropin (BST), a genetically-engineered version of a natural growth hormone found in cattle. The manufacturers claim that injecting cows with BST boosts milk yields by up to 20 per cent. Although BST has never been properly tested on humans, consumers in Britain and the US have already been sold unlabelled milk and meat from BST-treated cows when the synthetic hormone was undergoing secret field trials. At present, there is a moratorium on the use of BST in the EC, but the manufacturers are pushing hard to get the Commission to legalize its use.

Opposition to the use of BST is coming from those concerned about its health effects on humans and on cows. Despite assurances from industry and government that BST poses no public health risks, fears have been expressed that BST could suppress the human immune system and trigger breast cancer in adults. Treatment with BST may also mobilize pesticides (many of them carcinogenic) which are stored in body fat. There is further evidence to suggest that the use of BST may push cows beyond the point at which their bodies can respond and still remain in good health.[93]

However, the real question we should ask about BST, and other genetically-engineered "improvements" is: do we need them and whose interests will they serve? As far as milk production is concerned, the EC has long had a problem with overproduction, and currently limits production through the application of a quota system. Public health campaigners want to see a reduction in the consumption of saturated fats and therefore in the consumption of milk. The development of BST is clearly not a reflection of the need to increase milk production, but, on the contrary, a classic example of pressure to intensify production on the land, to satisfy no-one except the powerful vested interests of multinational companies.

## Global Integration of World Agriculture

A fifth set of concerns centres round the integration of Southern economies and farmers into Northern systems of agriculture.

Conventional wisdom would have us believe that Northern countries have developed their agriculture to the point where it is so efficient that huge surpluses are produced, whilst countries in the South do not even produce enough food to feed their own populations. This is used to justify the transfer of industrial agricultural methods to the South. The belief in "natural advantage" is further used to suggest that by opening up world trade, and allowing Southern countries access to Northern markets, and vice versa, everyone will benefit.

Yet the history of agricultural trade between North and South is one of exploitation. In agriculture, as in other sectors, trade is controlled and dominated by the North: those in the North make the rules, those in the North decide which commodities to export and which to import. Countries in the South compete not according to natural advantage on an open world market, but as disadvantaged players on the periphery of highly controlled Northern markets.

Europe, the US, and other countries in the North may produce large surpluses of cereals, meat, milk and other commodities, but they do not do so by relying exclusively on their own land area. Many depend on exploiting "ghost acres" abroad to grow their agricultural inputs and food. The Netherlands, for instance, depends not just on the produce from its own two million hectares, but on an additional 15–16 million ha in other countries:[94] the United Kingdom farms two ghost acres abroad for every one farmed at home. In total more than 386,000 sq miles of land in the South is exploited in this way (four times the land area of the United Kingdom).[95]

Ironically, those countries grappling with "surplus problems" would, if their ghost acres were removed, almost certainly have difficulty in providing for their own food needs without radical changes in diet. Intensive animal rearing is not an efficient way of producing food for human consumption (it takes 6.9 kilogrammes of grain to produce one kilogramme of pork) and, if Northern countries could not use land in the South as an integral part of their agricultural system, present patterns of production and consumption could not continue. Yet increasingly world agriculture is being restructured around Northern production systems.

The pig industry is just one example of a more general trend. In the Netherlands, swine production has shifted from farms scattered around the country to huge confinement operations located near the major ports. Feed grains, notably soybeans from Brazil and cassava from south-east Asia, are imported and fed to the pigs. The emergence of Brazil as a major producer of soybeans has involved tremendous social dislocation within that country. With soya being grown on 100,000 hectare farms, small farmers have been pushed off the land and are left trying to cultivate the strips between the big farms and the roads.[96] The process has resulted in landless peasants colonizing the Amazon regions, notably Rondonia, thus contributing to the problem of deforestation. Yet 90 per cent of the Brazilian government's funds for research are directed to export crops, and all loans from Europe and the US are to support the development of export crop production. Recently Bolivia has received $12 million from the World Bank to cut down rainforests and expand soybean production for the same international markets. In south-east Asia, EC policies, which opened up the EC to cassava exports, led farmers to shift their cropping mixes to favour cassava production at the expense of soil conservation. The legacy is thousands of hectares of severely eroded south-east Asian farmlands, whose productivity is severely damaged.[97]

Nor do the problems involved in the global integration of agriculture stop there. The result of all this imported food being fed to intensively reared animals is a 40 million tonne mountain of manure in the Netherlands, which has become an environmental hazard. Four-and-a-half million cattle, 14.5 million swine and 100 million chickens are producing at least twice as much manure in the Netherlands as can be recycled on Dutch farmland.[98] Meanwhile, nutritionists are trying in vain to persuade people in the North to consume less saturated fat, and therefore less meat. Insidiously though, the Northern diet, with its high reliance on animal products, is spreading to the South.

Providing incentives for the best land in the South to be used for growing export crops for the North does nothing to aid the development of sustainable agricultural systems either in the North or in the South. The Northern agricultural system requires around 0.4 to 0.6 ha of arable land per person, yet the UN Food and Agriculture Organisation (FAO) has worked out that by the turn of the century only 0.15 ha of arable land will be available for each person.[99] Under these circumstances, it is not possible to justify the use of productive land in the South to prop up an unsustainable animal production and consumption system in the North. In reality, it is the North that is failing to feed itself from its own resources.

Yet global dislocation in agriculture has reached such a state that at the same time as Northern countries import vast quantities of animal feed and other commodities, they also grapple with their own "over-production" problems. As the pressure on farmers in the North to increase output has become greater and greater, surpluses have been generated, and the competition between countries for export markets has also intensified. Faced with the choice of paying for ever greater stocks of food to be kept in storage, actually destroying stocks of food, or subsidising the export of food to other countries, the European Community has chosen the latter course of action — as has the US, though less directly. As prices within the EC are 20–25 per cent higher than world market prices, substantial export subsidies are required if surpluses from the EC are to be disposed of on world markets. This policy has made the EC's Common Agricultural Policy — and European farmers — unpopular with farmers outside the EC who are affected by such dumping, and with European taxpayers and consumers, by whom the direct costs are borne.

As a result of export dumping, chiefly by the US and Europe, world market prices for many commodities are now well below the cost of production for even the most efficient producers.[100] This has caused serious problems for those trying to compete on the world market without the benefit of export subsidies, and for the domestic economies of many Third World countries. In a world where dumped food can be bought more cheaply than local farmers can produce it, the livelihoods, and lives, of many millions of small producers are being seriously threatened. The percentage of US farm products destined for export increased from about 10 per cent in 1960 to 28 per cent in 1980.[101] During the decade from the mid-1970s to the mid-1980s, the EC also considerably increased its exports of animal feed, wheat, beef, barley, wine and butter.[102]

Although proponents of free trade argue that if agricultural restrictions were removed, Third World countries would gain greater access to markets in the North, the evidence suggests that increased integration of world agriculture encourages the development of even less sustainable systems. In particular, if an agreement is reached under the General Agreement on Tariffs and Trade (GATT) which prevents countries from protecting their own farmers from competition with dumped commodities, or prevents them from fostering more sustainable systems of agriculture and keeping out food which does not meet their own standards, the effects will be very damaging. As global agricultural systems become a reality, the advantages are accruing not to those with "natural advantage", but to those with the power to control trade.

## Wider Threats

A sixth set of concerns relates to the threat to agriculture posed by the growth of industrial society.

### Paving Over

As industrial society expands, the loss of agricultural land to industry and urbanization increases, threatening the livelihoods of farmers and destroying the very food-producing base of society. In the US, three million acres a year are lost to housing construction, commercial and industrial development, water projects, lakes and highways.[103] In England and Wales, between 1933 and 1976, one-and-a-quarter million acres of farmland (30,000 acres a year) were lost to urbanization.[104] In the five years between 1975 and 1980, the average yearly loss of agricultural land to development or other uses in England and Wales alone was 45,800 acres.[105]

In all probability, the true extent of the problem is far worse than the official figures suggest. One reason is that government statistics are generally a tally of the net loss of land to urbanization and thus give no indication of the *quality* of the land lost. In Britain at least, land being lost to urbanization tends to be the good quality agricultural land surrounding the cities, while that being brought into production in its place is land with marginal potential for agriculture, but with high wildlife, landscape and amenity value.

## Global Warming

The expansion of industrial society is leading directly to climatic change and to the disruption of the atmosphere. Global warming and ozone depletion — once the stuff of science fiction but now a reality — directly threaten the productivity of agricultural lands and the capacity of society to feed itself in the future. Although the principal sources of greenhouse gases lie outside agriculture, agriculture's increasing dependency on fossil fuel — to power machinery, to produce fertilisers and pesticides, to transport produce to consumers, and to process food — means that it too cannot escape responsibility for global warming. To produce one tonne of nitrogenous fertiliser requires the energy equivalent of six barrels of oil.[106] Currently, 1.5 million tonnes of nitrogen fertiliser are used every year in Britain alone.[107] In the US, food production increased by a factor of two between 1947 and 1979, but the input of fossil energy increased by a factor of ten.[108] Today, US agriculture uses on average 10 kilocalories of non-edible fossil fuel energy to produce 1 kilocalorie of edible food.[109] If all the food in the world was produced in such an energy intensive manner, the known world petroleum reserves would be exhausted within just 13 years.[110]

Global warming is likely to make the main cereal growing areas of the USA and the USSR drier and warmer. Some areas will become so arid that rain-fed agriculture will no longer be possible. One-third of the rain-fed farmland in the western USA, for example, could be lost to production. Warmer temperatures may also increase the potential for pest infestations

— pests no longer being killed off by winter frosts — whilst the predicted increase in the severity and frequency of storms is likely to wreak havoc with today's vast expanses of monoculture.

If drastic emission reductions are not made — with cuts in the order of 90 per cent for carbon dioxide emissions in the Northern industrialised countries — temperatures are likely to continue rising until the planet becomes uninhabitable. Climatologists give their estimates for global warming in terms of the temperature increase caused by the doubling of carbon dioxide — the much quoted figure of 1.5–4.5°C — but temperatures will not reach these levels and then stop. They will go on rising and the accompanying changes in rainfall and other factors will also continue.

Farmers will be faced with a situation where the weather of the last few years will not be a guide to the weather of the next. They will not know what crops to plant, or when they should be harvested. Those who put their faith in more scientific research fail to understand the limits of forecasting the behaviour of a system as complicated as the atmosphere. Climatologists can predict that the climate will change, but they cannot provide farmers with accurate yearly models of how much the change will be and what it will mean in terms of rainfall, windspeed and sunshine.[111]

## Ozone Depletion

Stratospheric ozone depletion is leading to increased exposure to ultra-violet B radiation at ground level, posing a major threat to crop yields. Many plant species, including peas, beans, cabbage and certain varieties of soybean and wheat, are sensitive to UV radiation. Reduced growth and nutritional value, and increased susceptibility to disease are some of the effects of exposure to high UV levels.

## Chapter Two

# Pushed onto the Treadmill

Confronted by mounting evidence as to the environmental destructiveness of industrial agriculture, and increasingly unable to avoid discussion of its social impacts, mainstream agronomists and policy-makers have belatedly recognized the need for change. "Sustainable agriculture" has become the buzz word of the moment.

But "sustainable agriculture" means all things to all people. To the British Treasury, for example, it means agriculture which the tax-payer can afford. To the agrochemical industry, it means eliminating the most controversial pesticides and, increasingly, adopting the new genetically-engineered crops. The question therefore arises: sustainable agriculture for whom? Whose interests are we seeking to sustain? And to the detriment of whom?

To answer those questions means going beyond a narrow — and frankly sterile — debate on the technologies that might make for a more "sustainable agriculture" and confronting instead the political and economic forces that have driven farmers into agriculture's present disastrous cul-de-sac.

## Deliberate Policy

It is traditional in the West to look back over human history as a steady but inevitable march of social improvement. The line from hunter–gatherer to agriculturalist and city dweller and now to space-age technologist is frequently portrayed as a regional sequence of events which could not have been otherwise.

In agriculture, that notion of "historical progress" is invoked both to legitimise existing policies and to push those policies in the direction that most favours those who have benefitted from the status quo: it is also used to denigrate those who would seek change. For example, in 1991, Britain's Minister of Agriculture, John Gummer, pilloried proposals put forward by the EC Commissioner for Agriculture, Ray MacSharry, to target financial support under the Common Agricultural Policy (CAP) to family farms, in order to stem rural depopulation and promote rural development. The proposals, argued Gummer, would "turn farms into museums" and "make farmers curators of an increasingly outdated structure".[1] But most damning of all, by penalising large, intensive, farmers — "those who had invested, improved and won a better place in the market" — and subsidising "the small and inefficient", they would "hold up the natural changes that have been a feature of farming ever since it began". As Gummer put it to the House of Commons:

> "One cannot bribe people with more and more money every year to stay on wholly uneconomic plots. The MacSharry proposal is wrong in its fundamental principle. It does not face the fact that agriculture has been developing ever since it started and that people have been leaving the land, even in those countries that have done a great deal to support the smallest of farmers, such as we have not seen in this country for a century."[2]

Whilst it is certainly true that the modern era has seen high rates of rural depopulation — with Britain losing more than half of its farming population since the Second World War,[3] and whilst that depopulation has been accompanied by the spread of modern, intensive farming, it is quite false to suggest that such changes in farming and rural life have been the result of a "natural process", or that the transformation of agriculture has followed the path that it has by accident. On the contrary, farmers have, throughout the western world, been deliberately encouraged — indeed, in many cases, forced — into intensifying their operations. Despite the differences between climate, soils, farms, governments, and types of agriculture, the same pattern emerges time and again.

## The British Example

In Britain, farmers were virtually self-sufficient in farm inputs prior to the Second World War. Such machinery as existed on the farm was made locally or on the farm itself; draft power was provided by horses, raised on the farm and fed from the farm; and seeds were saved from one harvest to the next. Soil fertility was maintained through crop rotations and through rotating crops with livestock, the manure from the animals being used to fertilise the land. Typically a field might be used to grow wheat, then turnips, then put down to grass interplanted with legumes such as clovers and vetches, and then used as pasture. The planting of legumes was critical to the cycle, since legumes (unlike other plants) have the ability to fix nitrogen from the air and pass it into the soil through their roots.

Crop rotations also helped to combat pests, particularly those pests that are carried by soil organisms. Most pests and crop diseases are specific to individual plants and will not attack other species; a fungus that might devastate potatoes, for example, will not affect beans. If potatoes are grown on the same patch year after year, the fungus is provided with a permanent source of food and may quickly become established as a major pest. But if the potatoes are moved to another field and beans are grown instead, the fungus is not given an opportunity to establish itself.

In the late 1930s, however, the government set out to increase output by intensifying agriculture. With a war looming, and Britain dependent on imports for 60 per cent of its food, government thinking was heavily influenced by memories of severe food shortages during the 1914–18 War, when Britain was brought to the brink of collapse through Germany's blockade on shipping. Initially, inducements to farm more intensively came in the form of grants. In 1937, a scheme was introduced to subsidise the spreading of lime and basic slag on agricultural land to build up soil fertility. In addition, the government offered a subsidy of £2 for every acre of grassland brought under the plough, with the aim of bringing more than 1.5 million acres of land previously used as permanent pasture into production in the 1939/40 season alone.[4] During the War, food production targets were set for each county and further subsidies were introduced to encourage farmers to improve drainage and to adopt chemical controls on pests and animal and plant diseases. Extra fuel rations were allocated to farmers with tractors and to fertiliser manufacturers.

After the War, the drive for increased production continued. In August 1947 a programme designed to raise net agricultural output by 20 per cent over the next five years was announced.[5] Priority was given to expanding the numbers and output of livestock and the acreage under cereals and potatoes, and the range of subsidies and other inducements to encourage farmers to adopt industrialised methods of agriculture was broadened. These included:

- Subsidies for Fertilisers;

- Subsidies for Fuel;

- Subsidies for Drainage;

- Subsidies for Hedgerow removal;

- Preferential rates for farm borrowing;

- Free advice for those adopting intensive methods;

- A massive research programme into high input/high output systems.

The drive for increased production was given focus through the setting of targets. The 1947 Agriculture Act required farmers to comply with "rules of good husbandry". "Good husbandry" was often interpreted as maximizing output from the land, and failure to do this could lead to a supervision order by the county executive committee, and ultimately to a notice to quit. Between 1947 and the repeal of these provisions in 1958, 5,000 farmers were placed under supervision orders and 400 were dispossessed.[6] One individual was reported for failing to maximise production from chalk downland — an area which today conservationists are fighting to protect.[7]

Similarly, farmers were urged to invest in farm machinery. Investment of this kind, which usually involved borrowing, reinforced the need for increased output in order to service the loan. Grant and price-induced developments, encouraged by the National Agricultural Advisory Service and the manufacturers of farm machinery and chemicals, led to more farm specialisation and expansion, and the shedding of labour. Through the system of tax incentives, farmers were further encouraged to plough back profits into mechanisation and expansion.[8]

In the 1957 Agriculture Act, a new dimension was added to the cost-price squeeze. The Act laid down that annual price awards need not reimburse farmers for all the increases in their costs of production, as they should be expected to absorb a proportion of these each year through increases in efficiency. In other words, farmers who did not succeed in increasing their output each and every year could expect their incomes to decline.[9]

The knowledge that food prices would continue to fall in real terms year after year was the final nail in the coffin of many farmers who had attempted to avoid being sucked onto the chemical treadmill. Increasing output year after year was the only way to survive. As Philip Lowe and his colleagues note in their book *Countryside Conflicts*:

> "The farmer was required in effect to run up the down escalator; only if he could run faster than the escalator would he remain solvent or increase his profits. Caught in this cost-price squeeze, farmers had little option but to take up the grants on offer and to invest capital in new buildings, plant and machinery, to adopt new technologies, to make use of hitherto unproductive land, to remove any features that stood in the way of maximizing production, to dispense with much of their labour force, and to concentrate production in larger units — in short to carry through the second industrial revolution. Those who did so prospered. Those who could not went under."[10]

Britain's entry into the European Community and its subsequent participation in the Common Agricultural Policy did little to reverse the trend towards intensification. Drawn up at a time of relative food scarcity, the objectives of the CAP were:

- to increase agricultural productivity;

- to ensure a fair standard of living for the agricultural community;

- to stabilise markets;

- to assure the availability of supplies; and

- to ensure that supplies reach consumers at reasonable prices.

To achieve these objectives, the EC set up a system of paying farmers a guaranteed price for commodities which could not be absorbed by the market. This measure was designed to maintain farm incomes and provide stability in the agricultural market. The original intention was that such a scheme would be self-regulating, with stocks being bought into "intervention" during times of surplus and released back onto the European market during times of shortage.

However, the CAP's mechanisms for supporting farmers — principally price support — are linked to volume of output and have therefore benefitted large and intensive farmers disproportionately. Moreover, the structure of grants under the CAP has, in the words of EC Commissioner Ray MacSharry, "preserved a permanent incentive to greater production and further intensification".[11] Because subsidies are paid per unit of output and per head of livestock, the more that a farmer produces and the greater the number of animals raised, fattened or sold, the more money received. Inevitably, the CAP has encouraged farmers — and this applies as much to continental Europe as to Britain — to use their land intensively.

Ironically, given the CAP's original intention of supporting marginal farmers, the EC's attempts to solve its agricultural surplus problems by lowering guaranteed prices to farmers have hit small farmers, farmers in marginal areas, and those who are highly-borrowed, hardest. Farmers in these categories are being forced off the land, while those that remain are looking at ways to increase output in order to remain solvent.

## The French Example

Despite having the second largest average farm size in Europe, the French have not gone nearly as far down the route of intensification and farm amalgamation as the British. In 1983, when the average farm size in Britain was 170 acres, in France it was 63 acres. In Britain 2.3 per cent of the workforce is engaged in agriculture, in France the figure is 9 per cent.[12]

The reasons for the perseverence of small farms in France are both historical and cultural. After the French Revolution the peasantry benefitted from the redistribution of land and the abolition of numerous taxes and impositions. Any tendency toward the amalgamation of farms was counteracted by the replacement of primo-geniture with a hereditary system that divided the inheritance equally between siblings. In France the favourable attitude towards the "paysan" contrasts strongly with the British situation where "peasant" is a term of abuse, and large "efficient" farmers are held up as models to be emulated.

The French enthusiasm for good (though not necessarily healthy) food is also lacking in Britain. Many French consumers will go out of their way to buy food that is fresh, in season, and local. Agricultural products are strongly identified with a particular area. Prunes are intrinsic to Agen, lentils to Le Puy, Camembert to Normandy and Muscat to Lunel, in a way that is difficult to understand for those who dine on New Zealand Cheddar and Californian Burgundy. A visitor to another region in France will be sure to bring home a sample of the local *specialité*. Through this consumer loyalty to local brands, local producers are protected to a degree from the competition of cheap imports.

The consequence is the survival of local outlets that accommodate the small scale farmer. Producer-owned stalls are given priority at the weekly markets; shops stock regional wines and vegetables; and thousands of agricultural co-operatives, vigorously championing the village produce, offer a secure market, and an outlet to the urban hypermarket economy to farmers whose land falls within their circumscription. The local network offers part-time and retired smallholders the opportunity to derive a supplementary income from a hectare or two of land, and allows full-time farmers and stock-breeders to make a modest living from as little as 5 hectares of vines, 40 goats, and 100 milking sheep.[13]

In some parts of France, the smallholdings and traditional approach to agriculture have persisted better than others. In areas where commodities are mainly traded locally, the Common Agricultural Policy has had less of an impact than in areas concentrating on commodities like grain which are traded outside the area. However, despite the surplus problems within the EC, created by large intensive farms, the French government is now targeting policy on the small "inefficient" holdings. Long-term policy is to amalgamate small holdings into larger units; but since the agricultural sector wields a significant portion of the vote, the government has had to tread carefully.

Subsidies and grants, for example, are available to all registered farms, and additional subsidies are given to those in mountain areas. However, a further range of grants relating to the major improvement of land and facilities is only available to much larger farms, giving them a long-term competitive advantage. In wine-growing areas, grants for replanting are withheld if new vines are not planted in line with those in an adjacent vineyard, with a view to future amalgamation. Another instrument by which farmland is gradually regrouped is the SAFER. This organisation ensures that when any plot of agricultural land comes up for sale, priority is given to adjacent landowners.

However, without doubt the most far-reaching approach to amalgamating and "modernising" farms has been the policy known as *remembrement*.[14] To appreciate the way the French government has succeeded in playing off the different sections of French peasantry against each other, it is necessary to understand the decentralized structure of French society. The basic unit of rural local government is the *commune* — usually a village and its lands — which is administered by an elected mayor and council. Their powers are much greater than those of a parish council in England and extend, in practice, to such areas as water supply, road maintenance and planning permission. There are some 36,000 communes in France, some of which have as few as 25 voters. There is thus a significant measure of village autonomy. However, councils are susceptible to control by a clique, or may become the arena for acrimonious feuding.

Under a law that dates back to the Vichy regime of 1942, the government has encouraged the establishment of *commissions de remembrement* to administer the redistribution of land within a commune, or within a small group of communes. The committees are headed by a magistrate, and composed of two officials appointed by the Prefecture, five farmers from the commune appointed by the regional Chambre d'Agriculture, five landowners elected by the local council, and a "person qualified to oversee the protection of nature" (PQPN). These committees are empowered to survey and seize small plots of land and redistribute them to landowners who either have adjacent property, or who could ostensibly make better use of the land. Ideally, the commissions are supposed to ensure a fair exchange, mutually beneficial to all parties. However, since they are composed of trusted members of the local land-owning establishment, and unaccountable to the general electorate, they have a tendency and a state sanctioned opportunity to impose exchanges of property that are distinctly unfair. As Yann Brekilien, a magistrate who resigned from the presidency of a *commission de remembrement* put it, "magistrates have been placed at the head of commissions for the sole purpose of bestowing upon highly dubious operations a semblance of legal integrity. Beneath the umbrella of

Justice, technocrats and landowners can carry out the most underhand deals with impunity."

There is, of course, the right of appeal: a landowner who feels victimized can take the case to a regional tribunal. But the tribunal has no power to suspend the activities of the *remembrement* commission, and the authorities or the new owner of the contested plot can continue bulldozing, roadbuilding, tree-felling or hedge-removing, while the litigation is in process. Thus, although the court may finally, and sometimes after many years, find in favour of the aggrieved owner, the *remembrement* is a *fait accompli*, and the complainant can only claim damages. In effect, the French government, in Yann Brekilien's words, "has sown the seeds of hate" amongst villagers, and washed its hands of any responsibility.

Over 12 million hectares of land have been traded in this manner, mainly in the North of France (the vineyards of the South, which are only replanted every 25 to 50 years are less amenable to *remembrement*). Thousands of outraged property owners, who have been palmed off with a scrap of barren wasteland, or obliged to pasture their stock miles from their farm buildings, have filed complaints, many pursuing their litigation long after they have lost hope of retrieving their property. Several complainants, including a man of 83, have gone on hunger strike, and there have been dozens of cases of suicide by villagers, heart-broken at the loss of a treasured plot.

The regrouping of land involves considerable environmental damage. Trees, hedges and embankments are destroyed to provide bigger fields. In the single *departement* of Manche, an estimated 12 million trees have been destroyed. Some landowners have seen the trees that provided a wind-break for their home destroyed to provide a larger field for a neighbour. The creation of vast arable prairies has required the digging of correspondingly deeper drainage ditches, gouged into the landscape with a recti-linear disregard for its natural contours, sometimes draining the water table and drying wells. Yann Brekilien describes how the oak-crowned embankments in his native Britanny, constructed over centuries to protect fields against erosion from wind and rain, have been systematically destroyed: "Britanny has only become fertile thanks to the protection of these dykes. Pulling them down is not progress, but a return to the palaeolithic."

Since 1990, considerable public attention has focused upon *remembrement*, largely because of the campaign of one woman, Simonne Caillot, who has lived for nearly a year in a car parked by the monument of St Lô, Manche, and twice gone on hunger strike, to protest against the destruction of trees that protected her house. But demands for a government inquiry have so far fallen on deaf ears.

At a time of increasing frustration within Europe over the difficulties in cutting back on the production of surpluses, it seems ironic that the French government should have become obsessed with the need to modernise and rationalise production. This push towards larger and more intensive production is certainly not part of a "natural process of evolution", but rather the result of a deliberate policy to wipe out small farmers. Yet these small farmers tend to be more energy efficient than their larger counterparts; they are producing for a real, local market, rather than for intervention; they do not damage the interests of farmers in other countries, and they provide products that consumers actually want to buy.

*Remembrement* should be seen in the context of a drive to centralize the entire fabric of French society. The government also has plans to reduce the number of communes by two thirds, and to double the number of motorways across the country by the end of the century. Such schemes are viewed as essential to project France into the 21st century — but at the same time they are ravaging the environment, undermining the independence of farmers, and destroying a rich and varied culture.

## The Spanish Example[15]

Spain was one of the last countries to join the EC. After years of isolation from Europe under the Franco regime, becoming one of the privileged "club" was presented as the ratification, by fellow Europeans, of the triumph of democracy and freedom. Spain had at last become part of "modern" Europe.

In economic terms, joining the EC has turned out to be problematic for Spain. Industry is undergoing a difficult conversion, and in the process many small firms have closed down or been absorbed by big companies, most of them foreign. The agricultural sector has also been badly hit, as hopes for easy markets and advantages for Mediterranean products were dashed. Small farms in particular have suffered badly from CAP policies and pricing.

Before joining the Community, the protection provided by Spain for its traditional production had allowed farming economies to subsist in many areas. In northern Spain, where there is a mild climate and high average rainfall, the industrial areas alternate with green valleys and mountain areas, where the traditional basis of the economy has long been cattle raising. The family farms which concentrated on dairy products and extensively-reared, high quality meats, are now finding themselves unable to compete in their own domestic market with the produce from intensive dairy farms in Holland. EC milk standards give an added sting to the competition by favouring intensively produced milk with its low fat content. Already, rural communities and cultures in northern Spain, self-sufficient and prosperous until recently, are beginning to break down as a result of the competition from "efficient" Dutch intensive farms.

In central Spain, the two Castillas, the wide deforested plains with poor soils and an arid climate have for centuries been Spain's cereal granary. However, their low yields make it difficult for the Castellanos to compete with production in other European countries, so the future of local communities, practising their extensive system of wheat production, is under threat. Already dams are being built wherever possible, to hold water in order to irrigate the plains — possibly for intensive poplar plantations. An EC programme for improving the conditions of farming in Spain, approved soon after the country joined the EC, provided funds for new irrigation schemes, and infrastructure works, all directed towards the intensification of agriculture.

In Mediterranean Spain, agriculture is also suffering from EC policies. Olive oil and wine are surplus products within the EC, and there are incentives to abandon or uproot the old trees and vines. Olive oil in particular is now faced with competition from cheap vegetable oils which are a by-product of grains grown mainly for fodder for intensive livestock raising. In Extremadura, a 4 million hectare region in the southwest, the largest dam in Europe was recently completed, in order to provide irrigation for plains at present covered by vineyards and olive groves.

In the face of competition from intensive agriculture in other European countries, Spain is losing its small-scale, sustainable, agricultural production; its farming population is being forced off the land, its rural communities are disintegrating, and the environment is under threat. In the market place, delicious old varieties of apples are no longer available because the trees are being replaced with French varieties that provide a uniform crop and can be kept in central distributor fridges for much longer; the dairy farmer can no longer sell fresh milk directly, because of new sanitary provisions.

In Spain, as elsewhere, the only way for farmers to survive is to abandon traditional techniques, to expand and to intensify. But this is neither a natural process of development, nor merely the logical outcome of fair and reasonable competition.

After a period of being a net contributor to the EC, the Spanish government jumped at the chance of recouping its losses by obtaining funding for development programmes. The National Plan for Regional Development was rapidly produced, with little opportunity for consultation. The result is a development plan strongly biased towards large infrastructural works, the promotion of agricultural intensification, and mass tourism. Even when the regional details of the plan were being worked out by regional authorities, there was no attempt to involve local groups in consultation. It was difficult, or impossible, for local groups to get access to information before plans were approved, and even after approval, monitoring their implementation has not been easy.

The way in which EC funds are being used to promote macro-infrastructural projects and agricultural intensification, at the expense of the environment and local communities, is exemplified by the development of the Extremadura. In this sparsely populated area (the size of Switzerland), agriculture accounts for 30 per cent of employment, and traditional agricultural systems have, over the centuries, developed to interact with, rather than destroy, the natural environment. Fragile and generally shallow, poor soils and a climate characterized by a long summer season, with no rainfall, and mild winters with average rainfall ranging from 400 to 1,000mm, have set natural limits for agricultural activities.

In mountain areas and on steep slopes, very vulnerable to erosion, a dense Mediterranean forest with thick underbrush has been preserved. This land provides browsing for livestock (mainly goats), game, cork, honey, fruit, herbs, mushrooms, and, in higher rainfall areas, firewood and selective timber extraction. The areas are often communally owned, or privately owned and rented out to shepherds for summer grazing. In the plains there is a more savanna-like landscape called *dehesas*, where extensive livestock in a transhumance regimen allows for optimum use of pastures not only in the lowlands, but also in high mountain areas where only summer grazing is possible. *Dehesa* management includes careful pruning of trees to improve fruit yield (providing additional fodder in the winter months, and firewood for very high quality charcoal); improvement of pastures through grazing and continuous organic fertilisation; and shrub control. Tree regeneration is left to nature, but helped by shepherds, who protect young trees by simple methods such as placing dry thorny branches around them to discourage bruising of tender shoots. In the more fertile valleys further north, there is a concentration on fruit groves and family vegetable gardens, while to the south an ancient lake basin, now dry, is planted with extensive vineyards and olives.

In the past three decades, land use has begun to change. Traditional forestry, based on the multiple use of woodlands by rural communities, is being replaced with large timber plantation for logging, and local people are increasingly denied access to forest resources. In the development process, low quality timber is replacing hardwoods, and small family woodcraft and carpentry co-operatives are losing ground to larger, more mechanized industries. The species used to reafforest (pine and eucalyptus) are not suited to climate conditions and thousands of hectares burn every year in the summer season. Many of these fires are possibly started on purpose by country people who would rather see the timber burn in hope of gaining back their grazing land, or whose only benefits from the woodland are government wages for re-planting and fire prevention schemes. What work there is goes largely to outsiders: to bulldozer companies in charge of work on forest roads and firebreaks; to engineers who plan and direct operations; to chemical companies who sell pesticides; to the companies who own the helicopters and planes used for aerial spraying and fire control, and so on.

The intensification of *dehesas* has gone hand in hand with Spain's industrial growth in the last 25 years. As high quality farm products from *dehesas* lost their markets in favour of cheaper industrial foodstuffs, and as people began to drift to the cities in search of higher wages, thousands of hectares of Mediterranean woodland have been uprooted, and substituted with large irrigation schemes promoted by the government. Now, with encouragement from the EC, agricultural and forestry regional policies are totally geared towards industrialisation. The administration claims that the "modernization" process is needed in order to reach "development" levels of other "more advanced" European regions, and to promote job creation in the region. Investment is therefore directed at infrastructure works that have little to do with local community needs, and which cause severe environmental damage and loss of local resources and opportunities.

In Extremadura, the Regional Development Programme is not an "integrated" plan but a set of sectoral programmes. The *Programme for the Improvement of Farming* sets out as its objectives the intensification and mechanisation of farming, in order to create jobs in rural areas. None of the budget areas provide support for traditional extensive farming, nor for conservation of local breeds or traditional practices.

Investment is allocated as follows:

- *Road Infrastructure: 2,813 million pesetas.*
  Two thirds of this is allocated for the provision of new roads. Given traditional extensive uses of land, there is already an adequate road network, and new roads will damage the landscape and countryside without bringing any great benefits. The 840 million pesetas allocated for road improvement is justified, but there is concern that roads may be upgraded to a level far beyond the needs of local communities, and in the process cause more environmental damage.

- *Improvement of Irrigation: 1,534 million pesetas.*
  Existing irrigation networks are in many cases in a very bad state, and there is a need for investment in repairing the traditional irrigation systems. Approximately half of the irrigation budget is, however, allocated for extending the irrigation system. In some cases this means irrigating land where the possibility of irrigation had formerly been considered and dismissed, because the cost of necessary inputs was too high and profits were low or non-existent. Given the surpluses within the EC, and the pressure to reduce the budget, extending irrigation into areas where there is little hope of an economic return without subsidies makes little sense. The regional government is already subsidising energy (needed to pump water) in order to keep farmers on the land.

Extension of irrigation schemes into *dehesa* areas, where soils are poor and really unsuitable for irrigation, is both environmental and economic madness. One scheme has in fact been halted as it threatened to "improve" land which was recognized by the Environmental Directorate of the European Commission (DG-XI) as a priority site to be protected because of its valuable habitat. Unfortunately, where it is impossible to demonstrate a direct threat to a rare and vulnerable species of bird or animal, projects are almost impossible to stop.

- *Land Amalgamation Schemes: 412 million pesetas.*
  The dispersed nature of plots is one of the problems faced by small farmers, especially in irrigated areas. This scheme, however, seems unlikely to be managed in a sufficiently sensitive way to allow land holdings to be regrouped without damaging the environment. There is a real fear that in amalgamating land, natural features (brooks, uncultivated marginal areas, border vegetation and stone fences) will disappear with a disastrous effect on the environment, rural life and economy. The disappearance of countryside features that are linked to country life and cultural values, such as wild herbs and game species, could have a very negative effect on the economic and recreational opportunities for local communities.

The *Programme for the Protection of the Environment and the Conservation of Natural Resources in Extremadura* is no less technocratic, with investment allocated as follows:

- *Forestry/Reafforestation: 900 million pesetas.*
  This has effectively involved clearing existing maquis vegetation from slopes with heavy machinery, in order to plant evenly-spaced trees (many of which die soon after planting). This is going ahead despite the fact that maquis has long been used and managed by local populations, and provides valuable wildlife habitat for species such as Lynx, Imperial Eagle and Black Vulture. Under this plan, large areas have been "cleared" for reafforestation, exposing fragile mountain soils to erosion by rain and wind. The result has been losses of more than 20 tonnes of soil per hectare, and resulting problems with filling and pollution of watercourses. The alternative of planting by hand, without clearing the maquis, which could be very positive in areas where the forest has degenerated due to forest fires or over-exploitation, is approved by the administration in theory, but not implemented.

54

- *Improvement and Conservation: 910 million pesetas.*
  Unlike traditional systems of management, where forests were used and cared for by local people, the "modern" approach to forests requires finance for fire prevention, fire control works and reafforestation of burnt areas. Under the development plan, "cleaning" of forests is undertaken with heavy machinery, with disastrous erosion consequences. Instead of open communal grazing areas alternating with woodlands, to form natural firebreaks, the forestry administration favours the opening up of 15m wide firebreak strips in a checkerboard pattern, in spite of the evidence of their uselessness in case of fire, and their environmental cost. Like reafforestation, the conservation works rely heavily on contractors with large machinery, and provide little employment for local people.

- *Forest Roads: 144 million pesetas.*
  "Modern forestry practices", which involve the use of heavy machinery are used to justify the extension and improvement of the road network. In mountain areas with steep slopes the opening up of new roads (up to 30m wide) inevitably leads to an increase in erosion. The programme of road building, and associated forestry practices, which have obstructed or filled in the natural water drainage has triggered an increase in the incidence of "natural disasters" (floods) in recent years. Furthermore, forest fire hazard increases with provision of easy access to vehicles of remote areas of forest, as do problems of poaching and disturbance of fauna and free-ranging domestic livestock. Nevertheless, forest road work is accorded very high financing by the EC under community forestry support.

- *Erosion control: 360 million pesetas.*
  Traditional management which retained the vegetation cover and did not expose soils to unnecessary damage represented a good way of controlling erosion. Under the development plan, money is provided for: canalisation of the rivers; small dams for water regulation and terracing; and improvement of vegetation cover. All these projects involve big machinery and "high tech" solutions which are both unnecessary and inappropriate. Canalisation of the rivers degrades water quality, destroys important wildlife habitats and downgrades the visual beauty of the area, while contributing to, rather than preventing, erosion. The small artisanal dams which already exist provide a much

better way of channelling and using water than their proposed new counterparts which are bigger and much more destructive of the environment. Traditional terracing work in mountain valleys is a way of making good use of natural resources. The process of terracing with bulldozers — turning over soils and destroying soil profiles, removing all vegetative cover, and levelling out large areas — leads to the erosion of soil which had taken hundreds of years to build up.

The intensification of farming already taking place in the region means that aerial pesticide spraying, subsidised by the regional administration, is now normal practice, both for farmland and in wooded areas. The devastating effect on insect populations (including very rare and endangered species) has had a knock on effect for bird and amphibian populations which depend on insect life as a source of nourishment. The area is consequently becoming less desirable as a habitat for both fauna and humans.

The vast amounts of money being directed into agricultural intensification tend to undermine rather than improve, the economic and environmental framework within which local communities have to operate. Yet it is EC policy to encourage agricultural intensification and much of its Structural Fund is being devoted to this purpose. Nevertheless, the "efficiency" of straight-line engineering and big machinery is much more highly valued by planners and construction companies than by local people.

## The US Example

In the US, the pattern of intensification has also been one in which subsidies and other incentives have provided the main mechanism through which farmers have been encouraged to adopt chemical inputs and to mechanise their farms. As a 1989 report by the National Academy of Sciences notes:

"In more than half a century of operation, government policy has not only affected commodity prices and the level of output, but it has also shaped technological change, encouraged uneconomical capital investments in machinery and facilities, inflated the value of land, subsidised crop production practices that have led to resource degradation such as soil erosion and surface and groundwater pollution, expanded the interstate highway system, contributed to the demise of the railway systems, financed irrigation projects, and promoted farm commodity exports."[16]

Since the 1940s, US farmers participating in "federal commodity programmes" have received guaranteed prices for growing certain specified crops, a "deficiency payment" being paid to make up any difference between an agreed "target price" (laid down by Congress) and the going market price. Assured of a certain income from specific crops, farmers have been encouraged to specialise in growing the same subsidised crops year after year, rather than planting more varied (but financially risky) rotations. In 1989, over 70 per cent of US cropland was cultivated with crops eligible for price support — such as feed grains, wheat, cotton, and rice.[17] Deficiency payments made up a sizeable proportion of most farm incomes. The system has also encouraged farmers to strive for the highest possible yield on the greatest possible acreage, since the higher the yields, the greater the deficiency payment received per acre.

In the US, as in the EC, attempts have more recently been made to curb the production of surpluses through the manipulation of returns to farmers. During the period in which Reagan was in office, agricultural prices were cut by an average of 40 per cent.[18] Over this period another US farmer went out of business every eight minutes,[19] and those that were able to keep farming were often forced to intensify as a survival strategy.

Income tax policies have also significantly influenced agricultural practices and investment. Until 1986 and the passage of the Tax Reform Act, farmers could claim against tax for the depreciation of plant and equipment, encouraging them to invest heavily in new machinery and buildings. In particular, investment tax credits were instrumental in encouraging farmers to adopt irrigation and to set up feedlots.[20] Between 1973 and 1983, more than one million acres of sandhills were brought under centre pivot irrigation in Nebraska alone, farmers receiving $175 per acre in tax advantages through a combination of the water-depletion allowance, plant depletion allowances, and investment tax credits. The water depletion allowance permitted farmers to claim a deduction if they could prove that they were irreversibly depleting certain groundwater reserves.[21] Similarly, favourable capital gains provisions — under which

60 per cent of the profit from selling farm assets (including land and stock) can be set against tax — provided a major incentive to farmers to bring marginal lands into production. Farmers could drain wetlands, for example, sell at a profit, and claim the tax breaks. Farmers converting wetlands to cropland could expect to make some $603 per acre through such tax breaks.[22]

Overall, as the NAS study notes, much US farmland is now managed "to maximise future eligibility for farm program benefits" and tax allowances rather than to ensure good husbandry.[23] The result has been "heavier use of fertilisers, pesticides and irrigation than can be justified by market forces in any given year"; "the inefficient, potentially damaging use of inputs"; and a "surplus production of the same crops that the commodity programs are in part designed to control . . ."[24]

# Chapter Three

# Caught on the Treadmill

Squeezed by prices, encouraged by advice and training, controlled by regulation, limited by research, and trapped by peer pressure, farmers have had little choice but to adopt more and more intensive systems. The result has been a transformation not only in agricultural practices but, perhaps more significant still, in the political and economic landscape in which farmers operate, creating dependency where there was independence, driving farmers into a spiral of increasing debt, concentrating landholdings, undermining choice and increasing the vulnerability of farmers, entrenching old inequalities and creating new ones, disempowering smaller producers and consumers and shifting power to large farmers and corporations.

A number of interlocking processes, each reinforcing the other, lie behind that transformation. They include:

- Loss of control over inputs;
- Increasing debt;
- An increasing concentration of land holdings;
- Increasing corporate control over the food industry; and
- Declining bargaining power for farmers and consumers in the marketplace.

## Loss of Control over Inputs: The Road to Dependency

For the first time in history, the majority of western farmers no longer control their key inputs but instead purchase them from farm suppliers. Instead of using farmyard manure and judicious rotations to maintain fertility, for example, farmers now buy fertilisers in a bag. What was previously provided as a free "by-product" of good husbandry must now be purchased on the open market — a market over which they have no control and in which the limited bargaining power they do have is largely dependent on the size of their operations.[1] Similarly, instead of collecting seeds from one harvest to use in the next, farmers are now almost universally reliant on hybridized seeds, which not only demand large inputs of fertiliser and water to produce their optimum yield but also fail to breed true, thus requiring farmers to buy in new seeds every year.

The loss of control by farmers over their inputs would be of less importance if they were able to move in and out of chemical agriculture as they chose, without jeopardizing their livelihoods and at no cost to the environment. But such is not the case. The disruption caused by agroecosystems by pesticides and artificial fertilisers is such that farmers quickly become locked into a cycle of increasingly devastating pest infestations, declining soil fertility and diminishing returns on inputs. Unless they have the financial means (or are prepared to make financial sacrifices) to wean the land off chemicals and restore the natural processes that ensure fertility to keep pests in check without the use of chemicals, farmers have little option but to remain on the "chemical treadmill" (*see* Box opposite).

With the loss of control over inputs has come a dependency on the agrochemical industry — a dependency that the industry has been assiduous in cultivating. At first the agrochemical companies concentrated on the production of fertilisers and pesticides but, as part of the process of extending their control of inputs, they have increasingly taken an interest in, and come to dominate, the seed industry.

As Pat Mooney and Cary Fowler of the US-based Rural Advancement Fund International note:

"Diversifying into the seeds business was an obvious step for the petrochemical industry to take. Worried executives were aware that

# The Chemical Treadmill

Between the 1950s and the 1980s the use of agrochemicals in the Northern industrialised countries rocketed. In Europe, nitrogen use climbed from 50 million tonnes in 1950 to 100 million tonnes in the late 1980s, whilst, in the US, the use of nitrogen quadrupled between 1960 and 1981.

Pesticide use has also increased dramatically, as has the number of pesticides. As Chris Rose reports for Britain: "In 1961, there were 127 pesticide products in use in Britain, based on 14 chemicals. By 1985, there were over 3,000 products based on 420 active pesticide ingredients." In the US, between 1960 and 1981, the amount of pesticide active ingredients applied on farms increased 170 per cent, whilst the acreage under cultivation remained relatively constant.

The dramatic increase in the use of agrochemicals is due to a number of factors. Initially, impressive yields were gained through the application of nitrogen, potassium and phosphate fertilisers in a form which made the nutrients directly available to the plants. The increasing use of artificial fertilisers meant it was no longer necessary to rotate crops and livestock to maintain fertility, and with the development of a whole range of pesticides continuous monocropping became first possible, and then the norm.

To make the best use of fertilisers, scientists concentrated on breeding crop varieties which responded well to the application of large quantities of artificial fertiliser. Such varieties are costly to develop, and they tend to be patented so that the company could protect its interests.

As yields went up, prices came down, bankrupting many of those who preferred not to adopt the new package of seeds, fertilisers and pesticides. Those who adopted the new approach, however, stepped onto the chemical treadmill.

Getting off the chemical treadmill has never been easy. The cost-price squeeze which encouraged farmers onto the treadmill has increased rather than decreased in intensity. Farm gate prices have tended to fall in real terms, whilst the cost of inputs has gone up, with the result that farmers have to strive for higher and higher yields in order to make a profit.

Furthermore, in physical terms, the soil is damaged by the continued use of chemicals, and can take years to recover. The long-term fertility of the soil depends on more than the availability of nitrogen, phosphates and potassium: of critical importance are the levels of organic matter in the soil, the availability of essential trace elements such as magnesium, zinc and copper and the water retaining capacity of the soil. When a farmer stops applying manure and other organic materials to the land, and instead spreads artificial fertiliser by the sackful, the soil's structure gradually begins to break down. Without organic waste, the soil cannot support the micro-organisms that produce humus, and without humus the population of nitrogen fixing bacteria declines. The number of earthworms decreases (a problem made worse by pesticide spraying) and the soil becomes less well aerated, reducing the supply of oxygen available to soil organisms. The roots of plants become shallower as the nutrients in the soil become scarcer, thus weakening the plants. The soil's capacity to store water is also affected and the structure of the soil begins to break down, leaving the land prone to erosion and compaction — problems that are greatly exacerbated by the increasing use of heavy machinery and by monocultures.

To compensate for the soil's dwindling natural fertility, farmers must apply more and more fertilisers — but with the decreasing prospect that yields will increase. Indeed, in many areas, farmers are now confronting diminishing returns on fertiliser use. Twenty years ago, farmers in the US corn belt could have expected a tonne of fertiliser to add 15 to 20 tonnes to their grain harvest. Today the same tonne can only increase production by about 5 to 10 tonnes.

Pesticides too have the effect of trapping farmers onto the chemical treadmill. In part, this reflects the nature of chemical pest control. One problem results from the tendency of pesticides to increase (or indeed create) pest infestations by killing a pest's natural enemies: research in the late 1970s, for example, revealed that in California, 24 out of 25 of the major agricultural pests were so-called "secondary pests", their populations swelled to epidemic proportions because their predators had been destroyed by pesticides. In addition, many pesticides upset the natural metabolism of plants, causing proteins to break down, and making them increasingly susceptible to attack by pests.

Pesticide resistance compounds the problem. No spraying programme can ever completely eradicate an entire population of pests in one fell swoop. Inevitably some pests will survive and those that do are likely to pass on their immunity to the next generation. The list of immune insects lengthens year by year. In 1965, the UN Food and Agriculture Organisation (FAO) listed 192 resistant strains of insect pests; today, more than 440 insects and mite species and over 70 species of fungus are deemed resistant to the most common pesticides. Moreover, because resistance to one pesticide frequently confers resistance to others of the same chemical family, the problem can only get worse. Although chemical companies have sold the idea that without the use of pesticide crop losses would be devastating, there is little evidence to suggest that pesticides have brought major gains. In the late 1950s, insect pests destroyed approximately 7 per cent of US crops annually: by the late 1970s, insecticide use had increased 12-fold but pre-harvest losses had almost doubled.

growing health and environmental concerns would lead to a long-term reduction in the use of crop chemicals. But if farmers were to lose the crop protection and fertilisation afforded by agrochemicals, they could be persuaded both to increase the amount of seed sown and to become more reliant on new plant varieties. Buying into plant breeding and seed sales thus made excellent corporate sense, especially as seeds and pesticides require similar marketing systems."[2]

Following the example of large millers and grain traders, such as Rank Hovis McDougal, multinational pharmaceutical and petrochemical companies ranging from Shell Oil to ITT have moved to buy — or otherwise control — nearly a thousand once-independent seed companies, an indication of the importance with which such corporations now view the seed industry.[3]

In 1985, ICI, Britain's foremost chemical company, entered the market with the acquisition of Garst Seeds, a US company. Two years later, it snapped up the Société Européene de Semences (SES), one of Europe's largest seed companies for £93 million and, by 1990, its annual seed sales had reached £250 million. The company hopes to triple that figure by the turn of the century.[4] Unilever, the Anglo–Dutch transnational, is another company that has been assiduously building up its seed interests, buying the Cambridge-based Plant Breeding Institute from the British Government and Barenburg Seeds in the Netherlands. Unilever now ranks as the thirteenth largest seed company in the world, with annual seed sales running at $110 million a year.[5]

By the late 1980s, if the seed houses were ranked in terms of size, Shell, ICI, and Ciba–Geigy would all have occupied a place within the top ten. In Britain, three firms controlled nearly 80 per cent of the garden seed market. In the Netherlands, three companies controlled 70 per cent of the agricultural seed market, and four companies controlled 90 per cent of the market for horticultural seeds. In the US, one firm — Pioneer Hi-Bred — had tied up 38 per cent of the corn seed market.[6] Transnational seed houses now control about a quarter of seed sales in the North, and 5–10 per cent of sales in the Third World market.[7]

The strategy of selling inputs as a package has been pursued extremely successfully in the North. In the UK, Shell distributes free booklets with its seed varieties, indicating the optimum timing for the application of growth regulators, fertilisers and pesticides. Shell's spring barley varieties occupy over half the market, and its pesticides division has now developed an important seed treatment to combat loose smut in barley.[8] Another company, Dalgety–Spillars, which is a major force in breeding peas and beans, now offers direct advice on all aspects of dried pea production, including fertiliser and pesticide treatment.[9]

Since the early 1970s, seed varieties developed by companies have been patentable, making it illegal for farmers to trade in such seeds. Because of the problems of enforcing this, however, seeds are increasingly developed so that they do not breed true, or better still are sterile, so that there is no question but that the farmer must go back to the seed company for next year's crop. As more and more farmers are persuaded to change to the new varieties, the traditional varieties of seed quickly become extinct, reducing the genetic base of agriculture and increasing the vulnerability of farmers to pests and disease. The dangers of such genetic impoverishment were brought home in 1970, when a corn blight in the US threatened to destroy 80 per cent of the country's entire crop, and caused millions of dollars worth of damage.[10]

Within the EC, the loss of varieties is being even further encouraged by laws which make it illegal to sell varieties which are not "listed and approved" — the seeds falling into the non-approved category being almost exclusively traditional, non-patented varieties. In effect, the law operates to give corporations an effective monopoly over the supply of seeds by outlawing those seeds that they do not control.

With the advent of biotechnology, the control exercised by corporations over the farmer is likely to reach a stranglehold. Already, agrochemical companies are working to identify plant genes that will impart resistance to certain herbicides — usually their own brands — in order to sell seeds as part of a package deal designed to increase chemical sales. Worldwide, there are now at least 65 research programmes focusing on breeding herbicide tolerance into agricultural crops, with corporations like Monsanto, DuPont, Ciba–Geigy and Bayer leading the fray.[11] As Mooney and Fowler report:

> "The pièce de résistance in the package business is a triple cocktail being marketed by Ciba–Geigy. Two of the chemicals in the package are intended to control a wide range of weeds. The third is a herbicide antidote especially created to protect the seed from the two herbicides . . . The package has the 'advantage' that farmers must return to the company each year to have the antidote injected into the seed coating."[12]

In effect, the farmer will become totally dependent on the agrochemical companies.

## Increasing Debt

The higher costs of the new seeds and agrochemical inputs force farmers to seek higher and higher yields in an effort to repay loans and remain solvent. In Britain, pesticides alone cost farmers some £450 million a year, more than ten times the outlay in the early 1970s.[13] In the US, production expenses soak up 80 per cent of the gross income of large farms and 72 per cent of the gross income of smaller farms, leaving farmers with net incomes that, in 1981, were 30 per cent lower in real terms than in 1940.[14] According to the US National Academy of Sciences:

> "For many major commodities, fertilizer and pesticide costs far exceed other variable costs such as seeds and fuel. The national average cost of fertilisers and pesticides for corn production was about 55 per cent of variable costs and 34 per cent of total costs. For soybeans, the figures were 49 per cent and 25 per cent and for wheat, 40 and 23 per cent."[15]

With increasing costs has come increasing debt. In the 1940s, farm debt was negligible but today few farmers operate without a large, and growing, overdraft at the bank. By the early 1980s, the farm debt problem in the US had reached unprecedented levels, with total farm debt quadrupling from $53 billion in 1970 to $216 billion in 1983.[16] In 1982, interest payments on agricultural debt accounted for 98.9 per cent of net farm income. Even in good years, such as 1981, interest payments accounted for 66 per cent of net farm income.[17] Inevitably, the number of farms unable to meet their payments has risen sharply, a quarter of all farm loans in 1985 being officially classified as "delinquent".[18] In Britain, the problem is no less acute. By 1991 the main British banks had lent £10 billion to the agricultural sector and an estimated 70 per cent of net farm income was going to service this debt.[19]

Perched on a financial knife-edge, farmers are vulnerable to even the slightest fluctuations in the market or to minor set-backs in production. As Marty Strange of the Center for Rural Affairs, an agricultural policy research centre, notes:

"The expanded, more specialized farm has less slack and its margin of error is smaller. Stretched to the limit using specialized equipment to produce single crops for special markets; heavily indebted; dependent on a narrow range of particular inputs, especially energy and money; and deeply invested in sophisticated technology geared only to do one thing, produce more of the same ... these farms are economically brittle. When things go wrong they go very wrong indeed."[20]

Moreover, once in debt, the options open to farmers are limited: they cannot afford to restructure their operations if in doing so they run the risk of even a slight fall in income. In particular, the need to service loans is a major disincentive for those considering conversion to organic systems since productivity can fall sharply as the land is weaned off chemicals and fertility is restored: those with a heavy debt burden could not survive even a temporary reduction in income.

## Increasing Concentration of Land Holdings

Rising production costs — including the costs of borrowing money — and declining prices have had a knock on effect throughout the system. To earn a living, farmers must increase output, either by intensifying production on their existing holdings or by bringing more land into production, enabling them to raise more stock or to grow more crops. In Britain, for example, a dairy farmer in the 1950s could earn a living with fifteen dairy cows: by the 1980s, to have the same income in real terms, a farmer needed 75 cows.[21]

Encouraged by good returns, farmers (and others) who might otherwise have balked at the prospect of having to buy or rent more land succumbed to the pressure to increase the size of their farms. Indeed, in the 1970s, 80 per cent of all the land that came on to the market in England was bought by farmers expanding their holdings.[22] The result has been a steady decline in the number of farms and increasing concentration of land holdings in fewer and fewer hands. Between 1953 and 1981, the number of farms in Britain fell from 454,000 to 242,300,[23] whilst in the US the average farm size increased from 175 acres in the 1940s to 429 acres in the early 1980s,[24] with just one tenth of one per cent of the population — or approximately 240,000 people — owning half of the country's productive land.[25] A third of all output is now produced on a handful of "super-farms", the four hundred largest farms producing more than all the farms in Iowa, Illinois and Florida combined.[26]

Whilst good returns could be gained from farming, competition for land led to rising land prices, with farmers borrowing against the value of their land either to increase their holdings or to finance further intensification or both. But as farmgate prices have fallen back, land values have not held up and many farmers (36 per cent in England and Wales alone) now find they have borrowed more than the present capital value of their farms. Many have simply gone to the wall, their farms bought up at "distressed prices" either by other farmers or by corporations, or absentee investors.

Indeed, increasingly, those who work the land do not own it, whilst those who own the land do not farm it and, frequently, have no long-term interest in ensuring that it is kept in good condition.[27] It is simply an investment, to be farmed as intensively as possible in the short-term and to be sold to the highest bidder as and when the market is right. The trend is most apparent in the US, where large corporations (particularly oil and chemical companies) have invested heavily in land, creating vast holdings devoted to highly intensive monoculture. Such corporations — household names such as Dow Chemical, Monsanto, Union Carbide, Goodyear, and Coca-Cola — now own large areas of US farmland.

## Corporate Control of the Food Industry

The trend towards corporate ownership of land is paralleled by increasing corporate control of food retailing and processing. In 1986, over half of all food sales in Germany, the Netherlands, the UK and Belgium were controlled by the five biggest national retailers, the percentage of food sales controlled by supermarket chains in the UK alone growing from 63 per cent in 1976 to 83 per cent in 1986.[28]

Moreover, the trend towards concentration is speeding up. As Henk Hobbelink of Genetics Resources Action International (GRAIN) points out:

"Since the early 1980s, the major food processors have been involved in a life and death acquisition battle involving billions of dollars. Since 1982, a quarter of the 100 largest processors have disappeared into the hungry mouths of even bigger competitors. In 1985 four mergers, together costing over $16 billion, completely changed the US industry: Reynolds took Nabisco (formerly RJR Nabisco); Philip Morris took General Foods; Nestlé took Carnation; and Beatrice took Essmark. Later Kraft and RJR Nabisco — both in the top ten listing — were themselves taken over by the US buy-out specialist Kohlberg Kravis Roberts (KKR). Several others followed . . .

"'The food companies haven't finished eating' announced *Business Week* in 1989, with industry experts predicting that Europe's 45 major food processors may further merge into ten giant companies within the next few years."[29]

Increasingly, corporations are seeking to control food production "from seedling to supermarket". In Britain, supermarket chains such as Sainsbury already control each stage in the production of meat for their stores, from the animal feed through to the slaughterhouse, through a series of commercial ties with other companies. Similarly, Dalgety and Unilever —

two of the top five food manufacturing companies — now control 45 per cent of animal feedstuff sales, and both have interests in the seeds sector. Hillsdown Holdings, a major producer of red meat, bacon, poultry and eggs, has 150 subsidiaries and a turnover in 1987 of over £3 billion. Its poultry concerns include Buxted Poultry and Daylay eggs, it supplies its own feed from its own mills, and its own chicks from commercial hatcheries. Among its other concerns are 25 abbatoirs and several food processing, distributing and meat trading companies.[30]

In Britain, corporations have tended not to get involved in land ownership, but outright ownership of land or livestock units is by no means a pre-condition for controlling production. "Contract farming", in which farmers sell exclusively to one retailing company, growing crops or rearing livestock to their specification, achieves the same ends without the need to invest in land or stock. In Britain, within the last 15 to 20 years, contract farming has increased to such an extent that most of the poultry, eggs, pork and bacon, and over 90 per cent of vegetables like peas and beans are grown to the order and specification of the food industry.[31] In the US, less than 5 per cent of farmers farmed under contract in 1960: by the end of the century, that figure is expected to have grown to 33 per cent.[32] Indeed, in certain sectors, the figure is much higher: by 1980, 95 per cent of all broilers in the US were being produced under contract.[33]

Products grown under contract have to be produced to the right specifications at the right time. To help farmers with this process, specialist advice is given on what variety to plant, and the timing and application of chemical treatments. Farmers become mere cogs in the production system, and are effectively transformed into outworkers for corporations over which they have no control. In some cases, farmers have been reduced to virtual peons for food companies, their costs exceeding the money they receive in sales: in one US case, from the mid-1970s, poultry farmers under contract to Ralston–Purina, were found to be working for minus 30 cents an hour.[34]

Corporate control of the livestock industry is gaining pace so rapidly within the US that four companies now control 41 per cent of all poultry production, and three companies control three-quarters of all boxed beef production.[35] Battles are now going on over the hog industry, but it is not clear whether it will follow the poultry industry where the whole production process is controlled from feed processing to branded product, or whether, like the beef industry, control will start at the slaughtering stage. Four organisations also mill 52 per cent of the wheat flour in the US, and two organisations process 55 per cent of the soybeans.[36]

The result of such enormous growth in corporate power is that farmers have lost much of their control over the production process. As Professor Heffernan, a rural sociologist from the University of Missouri, points out with respect to the US broiler industry:

"The power relationship between the farmer, now called the 'grower', and the integrating organization had changed. Studies showed that growers felt they had no power in their relationship with the integrator."[37]

This sentiment was echoed by Christopher Turton, a British poultry producer: "It distresses me. I would prefer to be seen as a craftsman, not as a commercial exploiter of animals, but I feel I am being turned from one to the other . . . I am just a small cog in a big industry . . . Today poultry management is dictated by the company accountant rather than the stockman."[38]

## Declining Bargaining Power

With increasing corporate control over retailing, the bargaining power of farmers in the market has been severely reduced. Because of their enormous buying power, large corporations are able to trade in huge volumes of food and can drive down the prices paid to farmers, with the result that a decreasing amount of the total spent on food reaches farmers. Thus whilst food prices to consumers have remained more or less steady in real terms, farm incomes, particularly in the livestock sector, have declined substantially, and, in Britain, multiples such as Tesco and Sainsbury have doubled their operating margins.[39] In the US, the value received at the farm for food sold in supermarkets and grocery stores declined by 6 per cent from 1980 to 1987, with farmers receiving about $90 billion or 25 per cent of the $380 billion spent on all food — the rest went to the food industry.[4]

Increasing corporate concentration is also a hallmark of the international trade in major commodities such as wheat. Farmers now find themselves growing for a buyer's market, with multinationals such as the Cargill Corporation dominating the trade. As Peter Parrish, a cereal grower in Bedfordshire and a member of the UK Food Group, points out, "British (and world) wheat farmers are 'price-takers'. This means that the price of our product is not determined by the grower. Farmers, worldwide, take the price offered by the buyer." In Parrish's own case, the result has been a steady decline in real income:

> "The stark financial facts are these. In 1981, myself, and the vast majority of British wheat farmers, were making a return on capital investment of around 10 per cent. This was a similar return to what one would have obtained from investing in a building society. In 1991, I am receiving the same money for a tonne of wheat in actual terms as I was in 1981. At harvest, this was about £104 per tonne. In real terms, to enable me to reap the same reward as 10 years ago, taking into account the slight increase in yields during this period, my wheat should be fetching in excess of £200 per tonne, since all my input costs had inflated over this decade."[41]

By late 1989, Cargill controlled 15 per cent of the lucrative Ontario wheat market and independent operators charged that the company was effectively setting both the buying price and the selling price of Ontario grains.[42]

The increasing control of food production — from growing, through marketing to retailing — by corporations has a dynamic that is self-reinforcing. In order to stay solvent, farmers must expand their businesses and produce a greater volume of food. Large volumes of food can most reliably be sold through the multiples, and although this often brings a lower price, marketing and storage costs are reduced. Smaller wholesalers and retailers become starved of supply, and in many cases cannot obtain produce at the same price, so become uncompetitive, thus denying farmers alternative outlets.

Unable to compete with supermarkets, 95,000 food shops closed down between 1961 and 1983 in Britain alone. To put this in perspective, by 1979 there were only 67,550 outlets left, and within the decade between 1979 and 1989 there was a further decline of 34 per cent, with less than 45,000 outlets remaining.[43] In countries such as Germany, the Netherlands, France and

Belgium, there is a similar trend towards the dominance of large multiples, and the disappearance of smaller food outlets. In France, Germany and the UK there is approximately one food shop per 1,000 people, whilst in Portugal the figure is over four food shops per 1,000 people.[44] Inevitably, the death of the local economy connected to food production, processing and retailing has a knock on effect on other businesses and the provision of services, undermining rural employment in farming, local transport, processing and retailing.

Consumers are also losing out. Where consumers buy food direct from producers, or where the retailer is known both to the consumer and the producer, issues of food quality, methods of production and price have — to a large extent — to be negotiated. In some European countries, direct sales within the community are still an important feature of the local economy, but the trend is away from direct marketing. In the US, for example, the average food item travels 1,300 miles before reaching its final destination.[45] Inevitably, as the number of links in the chain between producers and consumers increases, so the bargaining power enjoyed by consumers is diminished to the point where, in many countries, consumers now have little or no control over what goes into their food or the prices they are charged for it. The result is not only a decline in food quality but an increasingly unhealthy diet — with the poor the worst affected.

Increasingly, the food that leaves the farm gate is barely recognizable once it has been transformed, processed and packaged for sale in the shops. This process is termed "adding value", and now accounts for a large percentage of the price which the consumer pays for the product. Despite the growing evidence that such highly processed foods are unhealthy, those on low incomes frequently have little choice but to eat them. One reason is that they are cheaper. Indeed, a study by the Hampstead District Health Authority in London recently found that the price differential between a "healthy" and "less healthy" basket of food items could vary by as much as 70 per cent over a week.[46] Moreover, at a time when consumers are being urged to consider the effect of their diet on their health, the combined weight of the food industry is making less healthy food (usually highly processed and with high "added value") even more attractive in terms of price. Indeed logically this is inevitable. Since the size of the market is fixed by the size of the collective stomach, the more fresh food that is eaten, the less processed food will be consumed. As it is the processed foods which offer the best opportunities for profit, the pricing policy is deliberately structured to encourage consumption of processed food.[47]

Thus, although the average cost of food to the consumer has increased little in real terms over the last decade, the difference in cost between less healthy items such as sugar and saturated fats, and more healthy items such as fresh vegetables and low fat products, has increased.[48] The multiples are further adding to the price differential with 28 per cent gross margins on fresh vegetables.[49] It goes without saying that a food system which makes highly processed food cheap and fresh food expensive, is not in the interests of producers or consumers; it contributes to the problem and costs of ill health, and benefits only the food industry.

The trend towards fewer and larger stores penalizes the poor, the elderly and the less mobile in other ways too. As part of their retailing strategy, the major multiples increasingly favour the development of large out-of-town hypermarkets. These hypermarkets stock the best bargains and the best range of products, but are most accessible to those who are mobile and affluent, while the sections of the population who would benefit most from the lower costs are those who can least afford to get to them. A single hypermarket can cost £30 million to build,[50] and its impact on the environment is significant. Each new site involves massive investment in roads and infrastructure, and grants and taxpayer's subsidies are not very far below the financial surface. The developments eat into unbuilt land surrounding towns and cities, and they suck investment, trade and daily life away from existing communities. The financial logic of the hypermarket is to capitalise on the new retailing technology, and there is a consequent loss of employment opportunities in the retail sector. For the consumer there is an appreciable loss of human contact, and a bias against those who cannot afford to buy and store in bulk. Significantly, the whole concept is based on the heavy use of the road system: to transport food from the farmer to the processor, from the processor to the hypermarket; and to get consumers from their home to the hypermarket and back.

## Chapter Four

# The New Barons

Inevitably, the major structural changes that have occurred as a result of intensification have rewarded some and penalized others.

### Large Farmers

At the farm level, the chief beneficiaries have been the large intensive farms, though different countries have different structures and therefore the beneficiaries are characterized slightly differently in each country. In the US, it is the corporate farms which have done best out of the intensification process; in the UK, it is the large grain barons; in Greece it may be the professional leaders of farmers organisations. Nevertheless, because the majority of farm support programmes are linked to production, those with the biggest farms have inevitably received the lion's share of payments, although, in comparison with smaller farmers, subsidies may make up a smaller proportion of their income.

In the EC, for example, 80 per cent of income support under the CAP goes to just 20 per cent of farms.[1] In Britain, the average income of large cereal farmers rose from £39,205 to £48,256 between 1983/84 and 1984/85; in the same period the average income of small dairy farmers fell from £3,903 to £3,633.[2] In the early 1980s, the largest 759 farmers in the Less Favoured Areas of England and Wales were receiving average headage payments of £13,000 per annum, whilst the smallest 11,000 farmers received less than £600 each.[3] In 1991, a leading Scots farmer with a farming empire of 50,000 acres was awarded over £500,000 in compensation when parts of his land were designated Sites of Special Scientific Interest, thereby restricting his ability to maximise his profits.[4]

In the US, the pattern is much the same, of the $9.3 billion spent on supporting growers of grain, rice and cotton in 1990, nearly 40 per cent went to just five per cent of the farms — those with revenues of $250,000 or more.[5] In 1982, the largest 10 per cent of the wheat farms received some 43 per cent of the government payments, while the smallest 10 per cent received just 1.4 per cent. Similarly, the top 10 per cent of the cotton farms received 40 per cent of the payments, with the bottom 10 per cent receiving 1.2 per cent.[6]

The system is doubly unfair; not only does it reward those who are already doing well out of the system (largely due to economies of scale) but, in doing so, it denies assistance to those most in need of support. The tax breaks available to farmers also operate to the advantage of large farmers, since small farmers with low incomes can neither afford to set aside money for reinvestment nor pay much tax. The largest farmers benefit in other ways too. Because they are the biggest purchasers of inputs, for example, they are able to negotiate special discounts that are not available to smaller farmers. Contract farming also operates to their advantage, since their greater output gives them an edge in negotiating prices with buyers. Similarly, where resources are scarce (as with water in the American Southwest), the bigger farms are able to use their financial muscle to ensure that they have adequate access to the resource.

## The Agrochemical and Farm Supply Industries

The agrochemical and farm supply industries have also gained enormously from the process of intensification. In 1946, ICI's sales to farmers came to a few million pounds; by 1982 the value of such sales was £1,350 million.[7] In the US, the total dollar value of the domestic agricultural pesticide market is about $4 billion a year. Herbicides represent the largest share of the market with a value of some $2.5 billion, followed by insecticides at $1 billion and fungicides at $265 million.[8] In 1991, companies such as Dupont and Dow enjoyed sales of $38 billion dollars and $20 billion respectively.[9] As with the food industry, the agrochemical market is dominated by a small number of major corporations, the top 10 companies controlling more than 50 per cent of total world sales in 1983 — a market then estimated at $13 billion.[10] By the early 1990s the global pesticide market alone was worth $21 billion a year.[11]

## The Food Industry

The third major beneficiary has been the food industry, or more accurately certain sections of it. Where vertical integration has been achieved — with large corporations, or related companies, controlling food production from the inputs to the branded products — the degree of control achieved over the food production process is staggering. In areas where this vertical integration has not taken place, it has been the large retailers which have steadily increased their power. Those supermarket chains which have not invested in farming, production or processing, supermarket chains have been free to respond to changing consumer demands simply by adjusting what they put on their shelves. The costs of any changes are always passed on to processors, manufacturers or farmers, and by making few commitments in these areas, and demanding high specifications, the supermarkets have minimised their risks.

In 1989 total expenditure on food and drink in the UK was £68 billion,[12] and the top twenty retailers of food in Europe had a joint turnover of £100 billion.[13] The largest retailing concern within Europe is the Metro group, with a turnover of over £7 billion; more than 82,000 employees; a sales area of more than three million square metres; and operations in Germany, Switzerland, France, the Netherlands, Belgium, Spain, Denmark, Italy, Austria, Turkey and the UK. As a group it operates a total of 142 supermarkets, 82 department stores and 46 cash and carry outlets, as well as other specialized units.[14] The next three largest operators in Europe are all French, with annual turnovers of over £6 billion, while the fifth largest is the UK-based Sainsbury, with a turnover just less than £6 billion.[15] In the US, the companies are different, though the picture is the same, with four companies accounting for 45 per cent of sales.[16]

As the power of corporations within the food production process has grown there has been much talk of efficiency and economies of scale. Professor Heffernan, however, maintains that these organisations are no longer concerned solely with efficiency and do not necessarily use their power merely to maximise profits. "More often they use the power to enlarge their share of the market or gain more control of other parts of their economic, social and political environment to assure survival of the organization."[17] Once they have achieved a certain degree of control, large corporations can then use their power to make sure that there is no longer a level playing field and they cannot be effectively challenged.

## Sources of Power

Large farmers, the agrochemical industry and the food industry now constitute the major power blocks in agriculture today, dominating policy to the point where what is deemed "good" for their interests is — in many circles — deemed to be synonymous with what is "good" for agriculture and food production in general. Their sources of power are multiple and, invariably, self-reinforcing.

### Success Breeds Success

Within the farming community, for example, the standing of large farmers springs in part from the perception that they are the most "progressive" and "efficient" force in agriculture — a myth that rests on a narrow, one-dimensional view of "efficiency" (*see* Box, p.15). In effect, industrial farming has come to be equated with successful farming. As Marty Strange observes:

> "The weight of community sanction is with the family farms that most emulate the industrial agribusiness model. They have 'progressive' images, considerable property (even if not paid for) that proves their worth, important friends, and most of all, political power. It is these farmers who get admiring stories written about them in the farm magazines, who win awards from small-town chambers of commerce (because they do a lot of business on main street) and who are considered top managers by agricultural experts. Their farms are on university tours and field days, seed companies want them to be their local dealers (for which they get their own seed much cheaper than the neighbours they sell to) and they are frequently elected to local school boards . . . They are prominent."[18]

Not surprisingly, it is the successful "industrial" farmers who are invited onto official committees, and whose views are taken most seriously by policy makers; they are also the farmers who are likely to have the time to be able to devote themselves to such policy-making. As Richard Body notes of Britain's National Farmers Union:

> "One might suppose that a national union of farmers would speak up for farmers of all kinds, and particularly for the small farmers who form the large majority. In reality, no one has any significant influence in the

NFU unless he is a member of its council. To serve on the council, a member must leave his farm to travel to London most weeks in the year and there sit on committees and perform other duties which are likely to take two or three days a week. Small farmers cannot do that: they are too busy sitting on their tractor or milking their cows. So the NFU Council has gathered to itself men less aware of the day-to-day realities than most farmers and less sympathetic to them. Being the large farmers — having 1,000 acres or more is not unusual for an NFU Council member — they have, almost by definition, been the beneficiaries of the system which has amalgamated tens of thousands of small farms. These are the men who have enjoyed the lion's share of the grants, subsidies and tax allowances; they have worked the system and they have prospered. Prosperity has blurred their vision."[19]

## Advisory Services

In the case of the agrochemical industry, the methods employed to push corporate interests are more direct. At the farm level, agrochemical companies have now established themselves as a major source of advice for farmers, complementing and strengthening their role as suppliers of inputs. In 1984, a survey carried out for *Farmers Weekly* found that although the British government's Agricultural Development and Advisory Service (ADAS) was well respected, "merchants' reps are more likely to be used for advice on day-to-day and other matters because they are often on farms anyway whereas the ADAS man would have to be called out."[20] The survey further revealed that the single most important subject on which advice was sought was the use of agrochemicals, with 61 per cent of farmers seeking information within a 12-month period. Needless to say it was the merchants' rep to whom farmers would turn for this advice, and it was the merchants' rep who was the first choice for advice on fertilisers, animal feed, new chemicals and crop innovations. Yet even those turning to ADAS for information would have been likely to have been given similar advice. Despite growing interest from farmers in the organic approach, it was not until 1988 that ADAS appointed an organic co-ordinator and a team of regional advisors.

## Advertising

The advisory role played by sales representatives gives agrochemical companies a powerful hold over decision-making at the farm level. That hold is reinforced through advertising in the farming press and in trade magazines, many of which are delivered free to farmers. In addition, the reliance of many farm magazines on advertising revenue from agrochemical corporations means that they are generally unwilling to bite the hand that feeds them. Cases of advertising being withdrawn as a result of articles which were even mildly critical of pesticides are legion.[21] As Graham Harvey, a British agricultural journalist, notes:

"In a number of cases, the agrochemical companies have shown themselves quite prepared to withdraw advertising *en masse* when they disagree with a publication's particular editorial line ... The weekly *Farming News* crossed swords with the manufacturers of the insecticide Temik over what the company considered an inaccurate and sensational series of articles on the product. Whatever the rights and wrongs of the articles themselves, the disturbing consequence was that a number of pesticide manufacturers withheld advertising from the paper, not just the aggrieved company."[22]

## Control of Research

Beyond the farm, the agrochemical industry has used lucrative research contracts and grants to establish close links with training colleges, universities and research institutes. Indeed, there are few agricultural institutions in either the US or Europe which do not now rely to some extent on industry funding for their activities. In Britain, the drive for privatisation, the reduction in public funding for research and the encouragement for near-market research to be funded by industry has reinforced the direction of research developments. The importance of such corporate involvement at the level of research and training should not be underestimated.

With funding comes control over the specific content of research projects. Industry is thus well-placed to suppress research that might rock the agro-industry boat. Bucking the system can result in demotion, ostracism by colleagues or, simply, the sack. Not surprisingly, there is a very human tendency for researchers to go along with what their funders require of them, even at the cost of compromising public health or the environment. As Henk Hobbelink notes of funding in the field of biotechnology:

"Monsanto has 'donated' $23.5 million to Washington University for biotech research; Bayer is contributing to the Max Planck Institute in Cologne for the same purpose; and Hoechst built an entire $70 million biotech research laboratory for the Massachusetts General Hospital where research on crop genetics is also carried out. Lubrizol has more than $20 million tied up in research contracts at 18 universities and other public institutions. These industry–university contracts have caused much controversy for obvious reasons. 'You don't need to know algebra to figure out how that committee works', says US congressman Albert Gore, talking about the committee that governs the Monsanto/ Washington University deal. 'No research can be done unless the company gives permission.' Of the Hoechst grant for a biotech laboratory, [one researcher has commented]: 'Essentially everyone in that lab is an indentured servant to Hoechst.' In most contracts, the TNC has the right to the first look at the results and can delay publication of them until patent possibilities are investigated."[23]

Although direct corporate grants to universities and research stations generally constitute a small proportion of total research budgets (with government providing the vast bulk of funds), corporate grants are an important source of power within research departments, particularly where a research department is otherwise underfunded. Corporate funding brings financial security to a project, conferring an "importance" which it might otherwise not deserve, and enhances the status of the researcher within the department. By a perverse logic, the capacity to "bring in" corporate funds becomes a route to promotion — with the result that key administrative posts within universities and research institutes have come to be dominated by those who share industry's priorities.

Because corporate funding enables researchers to "leverage" matching public funds from government,[24] even small amounts of corporate funding have a disproportionate influence on the wider orientation of public research. In effect, through the strategic placing of research grants, industry has been able to direct public funds into research that best serves its own long-term agenda. The process has, however, gained its own momentum and universities are embracing their own corporatist, profit-maximizing vision. In the US, public universities now allocate scarce resources to basic research which it is hoped will yield patentable processes and products to form part of the universities future endowment. The result is that biotech research for agriculture is being funded, while research work on ecology and natural resource management, which would bring broader social and environmental welfare benefits, is being neglected or eliminated.

Inevitably the orientation of research within universities and other public institutions filters through into the curricula of training colleges. In Britain, for instance, full-time education for students of agriculture or horticulture is free (funded by government) and courses on all aspects of industrial agriculture are readily available. By contrast, even today, the number of courses covering the organic approach is extremely limited. A few colleges now provide part-time courses in organic methods, and one or two private institutions provide longer courses, but no full-time training in the use of organic techniques is available either at agricultural or horticultural colleges or within the university sector.

With both research and training effectively dominated by the industrial approach to agriculture, industry is able to operate against a policy backdrop that is broadly sympathetic to its aims and views. With a common background and approach, those trained or employed in the mainstream can move freely between the academic sector, the public sector, the private sector and government itself. The result is a hand-in-glove relationship between the industry and its supposed regulators.

## Dominating Committees

That "revolving door" relationship between industry and the wider agricultural and academic community is most conspicuous in the make-up of the committees which decide on agricultural policy. In the Netherlands, over a third of the seats on the committee which decides on research funding for biotechnology have been assigned to commercial companies, with over half of these being controlled by the four top transnationals.[25]

Those who have close links with industry also dominate the committees that approve new techniques or chemicals prior to their being permitted on the market. Prior to 1985 and the passing of the Food and Environment Act, pesticides in Britain were "regulated" through the Pesticide Safety Precaution Scheme (PSPS) — effectively a "gentlemen's agreement" between the agrochemical industry and government, which would still be in place now had not the EC forced the UK to replace it with statutory controls. Whilst the civil service and the agrochemical industry were well represented on the PSPS advisory committee, consumer groups, environmentalists and farm workers had little or no representation. Moreover, the industry itself provided the data for assessing the pesticides. The bias of the system can be gauged from the decisions taken. By the mid-1980s, there were 41 pesticides on sale in the UK which were banned or severely restricted in other countries. 2, 4, 5-T which was banned in Norway in 1973, in Sweden in 1977, in Finland in 1978, and in the USA in 1979, is still in use in the UK.[26]

At the international level, too, industry's influence on such bodies as the Codex Alimentarius Commission (*see* p.108) is also considerable.

## *Lobbying Power*

Finally, all three of the groups that have benefitted most from the industrialisation of agriculture and food production have built up a powerful and effective lobby to promote their interests both within government and outside. Through the careful nurturing of personal contacts with politicians, civil servants, journalists and other opinion formers, reinforced through membership of the same clubs and through mutually-reinforcing friendships, lobbyists ensure that their voice is heard — and heeded — in government. Such contacts also ensure a steady and reliable flow of inside information to the lobbyists: indeed, it has been said (only half jokingly) that ICI — Britain's largest manufacturer of agrochemicals — has been known to receive cabinet papers before some ministers.[27]

# Chapter Five

# Undermining Alternatives

From subsidies through to research, training and the regulatory process, the bias in current policies is clear. Not only does that bias work to promote industrial agriculture but, just as important, it works actively to undermine alternative systems of production and distribution.

## Subsidies

The structure of subsidies varies from country to country, but the thrust is the same: large-scale and intensive farmers pick up the lion's share of taxpayers' money, and therefore effectively receive a subsidy for farming in a non-sustainable way, further disadvantaging those who are trying to establish or preserve alternatives to industrial farming. A case in point is the use of EC funds to encourage the adoption of "modern, intensive farming methods". In much of southern Europe, farmers are being given direct financial incentives to abandon traditional and sustainable practices (*see* p.49). As the markets for traditional produce are eroded, farmers get locked into a system of production and competition in which they need subsidies in order to survive.

The setting of target prices (below which the price for a crop cannot fall) tends further to discourage diversity and rotations, particularly where one or two crops become much more profitable to grow than others. In the EC, the high price of cereals has created a permanent incentive to grow them year in and year out, even on land that is barely suitable for cereal growing.

Providing support for every unit of output further militates against systems which produce lower yields, such as organic systems.

The US system not only provides general incentives for farmers to specialise, but actually penalizes farmers who reduce the acreage under subsidised crops, even for a short period, thus disadvantaging farmers who wish to rotate subsidised crops with unsubsidised crops. As the National Academy of Sciences notes, where price support payments are calculated as an average of the acreage under subsidised crops over a five-year period:

> "Any practice that reduces acreage counted as planted to a programme crop will reduce the acreage eligible for federal subsidies for the next five years. For example, if a farmer rotates all of his or her base acreage one year to a legume that will fix and supply nitrogen and conserve soil, fewer acres will be eligible for programme payments in subsequent years. In [this instance] benefits would be reduced 20 per cent per year for the next five years. Payment reductions would be even greater in subsequent years."[1]

Another rule, "cross-compliance" also acts to deter US farmers from diversifying crop production. Under the rule, farmers lose their benefits if they plant crops covered by a programme in which they are not enrolled. "The practical impact of this provision is profound", argues the National Academy. "For example, a farmer with corn base acreage and no other crop base acres would lose the right to participate in all programmes if any land on his or her farm was planted to other programme crops such as wheat or rye (oats are currently exempt) as part of a rotation."[2]

Directly and indirectly subsidies have had the effect of tilting the playing field in favour of the industrialised approach to agriculture. Unfortunately as traditional agricultural production and trading systems have been broken down, damage has been done which cannot be reversed by simply removing subsidies.

## Research Bias

Throughout the Northern industrial countries, governments have systematically underfunded research into alternative agriculture, disadvantaging farmers who have opted for organic and other environmentally-sensitive methods of production and discouraging more widespread change to alternatives. In the US, as Joel Solkoff, former assistant to the US Secretary of State for Labour, records, research aimed at "preserving the physical environment, encouraging rural community development and improving consumer nutrition" has been consistently discouraged by the US Department of Agriculture as being inimical to business interests. Instead, research funding has been directed into such fields as "reducing human labour in agriculture, and, in general, increasing agricultural productivity per unit of output", the exception being a short period during the Carter Administration.[3]

In Britain, government funding for agriculture is similarly skewed in favour of commercial interests. In 1987/88, Britain's Ministry of Agriculture, Fisheries and Food (MAFF) spent just over £48 million on agricultural research. Although reports now stress the Agriculture and Food Research Council's (AFRC) work on "lessening pollution, conserving the environment or improving animal welfare", the bulk of the funding for research is spent directly or indirectly on improving the "efficiency" of agriculture; "efficiency" in this context tending to mean improved productivity through genetic engineering, more efficient use of pesticides and fertilisers and new ways to improve yields. Indicative of the AFRC's approach are the following projects listed in its Corporate Plan for 1989–1993:

- Research into the timing and quantity of fertiliser nitrogen application to arable crops (£0.3 million);

- Identification of the direct killing effect of the herbicide paraquat on aphids (£0.1 million);

- Research into improving sprayers and the efficacy of pesticide chemicals (£0.2 million);

- Rationalization of fertiliser use of field vegetables (£0.6 million);

- Crop protection research on the size of spray droplets and the timing of spraying (£0.4 million).[4]

No research funds were available for research into organic systems, and those wanting to develop alternatives to the chemical approach were encouraged to fund their own research.[5]

More generally, an official reluctance to investigate problems related to the use of pesticides (and other aspects of industrial agriculture) has served to protect industrial interests from criticism, beguiling consumers and farmers alike into believing that the risks associated with chemical agriculture are too minor to be of concern. The pressure to change is thus reduced, as is the incentive to develop safer, more sustainable systems. The testing of pesticides is a case in point. Fully one-third of the pesticides on the market in the US are acknowledged to be inadequately tested, but although the Environmental Protection Agency plans a full review of the safety data on all pesticides, the review will not be complete before the turn of the century.[6] Nonetheless, the untested pesticides will still be permitted for use. In Britain, MAFF has plans to test about 250 long-established pesticides. These include various suspect items, such as maneb, mancozeb and zineb, three of the most widely used fungicides in agriculture. Lack of staff and funds means that the retesting will take about 40 years.[7] Meanwhile, such pesticides continue to be used.

# Regulations

Regulations do not only undermine sustainable agriculture by default. A number of regulations imposed by government actively discriminate against those wanting to produce food using ecological methods of farming. The following examples, drawn from Britain, the US and New Zealand illustrate the point:

## Milk Pasteurisation

In 1985, sales of unpasteurised milk through a third party, such as a shop, restaurant or health treatment centre, were declared illegal in Britain. Quite apart from reducing the nutritional value of milk, the new regulations, supposedly introduced in the interests of consumer protection, had the effect of blocking attempts by organic milk producers to develop direct marketing strategies, by forcing them to send their milk into a vast undifferentiated pool. Centres experimenting with the use of organic food as a treatment for ill-health were also affected. Since 1989, organic milk has been sold by Unigate Dairies and, more recently, by other companies, but to conform with regulations, the milk has to be pasteurised.[8]

## Compulsory Dipping of Sheep

The dipping of sheep to prevent the spread of scab is compulsory in Britain, and until the late 1980s the only sheep dips recognized by MAFF were those containing organo-phosphorous compounds. Such dips are banned under organic standards, because of the health risks associated with their use, and farmers opposed to dipping their sheep with them had to obtain an exemption from the Ministry, and then a manufacturer's licence to make up a lime/sulphur dip. Obtaining an exemption was time consuming, costly and difficult — MAFF itself admitting that "dispensation is unlikely to be given in areas at risk".[9] Today, the only commercially-available alternative accepted by the Ministry and the Soil Association (one of the main bodies developing organic standards in Britain) is a non-organo-phosphorous dip marketed by Bayer. Farmers wishing to use more traditional dips, or those who object to the practice of preventive dipping, still face considerable obstacles from the Ministry.

## Cosmetic Standards

In the US, many of the federal grading standards governing the marketing of fruit and vegetables are solely designed to protect against cosmetic damage to produce (blemished skin, for example) and have nothing to do with the safety or nutritional value of the food.[10] As the National Academy of Sciences notes, such standards not only actively encourage the use of pesticides in order to meet grading standards but are a powerful disincentive to alternative methods of pest control, since blemished foods command a lower price.[11]

## Marketing Structures

In New Zealand (where the Milk Corporation has a monopoly over the processing of milk) a group of large dairy farmers, interested in processing and marketing organic milk, secured backing from both major political parties to amend the Milk Act to allow them to do this. In an attempt to retain its monopoly, the Milk Corporation launched its own brand of organic milk, called "Naturelle". However, "Naturelle" does not conform to standards laid down by either of the organic certification bodies in New Zealand: it fails to require the humane treatment of animals, and has no concern for the effect of the farm on its surrounding environment. Despite complaints about this cynical approach to organic standards, the launch of "Naturelle" by the Milk Corporation seems to have been successful in heading off any change to the Milk Act, thereby undermining the development of genuine organic milk production and sales.[12]

In Britain, where the Milk Marketing Board (MMB) has the sole right to purchase milk, a group of Yorkshire farmers organized themselves into a co-operative and set up a dairy to process milk and sell it direct to the public. They had been advised by Brussels that the MMB only had powers over whole milk, not skimmed and low fat milk, and that therefore their operation was legal. In by-passing the MMB, the farmers were able to improve their profits by between £20,000 and £25,000 a year each, as well as providing milk to the consumer two pence a pint cheaper. The MMB, however, began to threaten legal action and fines of up to £1,000 a day. Intimidated by the MMB, the co-operative sold the dairy to a big food manufacturer, Northern Foods, and it was closed almost immediately with a loss of 60 jobs. The EC is now challenging the MMB's actions, but the Minister of Agriculture, John Gummer, has come down firmly on the side of the MMB.[13]

## Making Life Difficult

As well as these direct examples of the way in which regulations can be used to stop the development of alternatives, there are numerous ways in which regulations can make life more difficult and more costly for small, less intensive farmers. Having encouraged the development of industrialised farming with its disturbing implications for health and for the environment, governments often regulate in an attempt to limit the damage. In these circumstances, the costs are usually borne by the producer, and are most onerous for small producers. For example, the costs associated with testing for salmonella in poultry units, the testing of water quality on farms, and the building of slurry storage systems to prevent environmental damage (all of which are now, or are going to be, compulsory in Britain) represent a much bigger problem for small-scale producers than for big ones. The fixed costs imposed by these regulations exacerbate the economies of scale and further disadvantage small, less intensive producers.

# The Power of the Supermarkets

Farmers trying to rebuild the links between producers and consumers by marketing their food locally have, to a large extent, been thwarted by the erosion of local or regional marketing channels. By undermining the network of small wholesalers and retailers, and placing themselves between producers and consumers, supermarket chains in countries like Britain have achieved a position in which organic and other producers have little option but to market their produce through them.

The supermarkets demand high cosmetic standards and an enormously wasteful approach to overwrapping and packaging. With few established organic packhouses and processing plants, organic food is transported across the country to collecting and processing plants and then many miles more to supermarkets around the country. The "grade-out" of perfectly edible produce which fails to meet supermarket cosmetic specifications can be as high as 50 per cent,[14] and for fresh food the multiples' gross margin jumps from around 7 per cent to around 28 per cent.[15] The result is that returns for organic producers are low, while costs to consumers are high, which effectively undermines the organic market from both ends. Added to this, as supplies of organic produce increase, the bargaining position of organic producers is eroded, and, like conventional producers, organic producers are finding themselves being squeezed financially by the supermarkets.

Perhaps even more serious is the effect that selling to the multiples has on the actual production of food. Supermarket chains want precise amounts of produce at precise times and organic growers are under intense pressure to reduce the variety of crops they grow and to grow larger volumes of the few crops they can grow best. As they have to meet specific production dates, they are forced to plant not when weather and soil conditions are right, but on prearranged dates. Worse still, as the price squeeze begins to bite, there is less room for manoeuvre within rotations, less scope for fertility-building breaks in cropping, less time to deal with weed problems, and more pressure to buy in manure in order to keep up output. In short, organic producers are being manipulated onto the same treadmill that conventional producers have been on for some time — a treadmill that benefits neither producers nor consumers.

Nor does this process affect only organic producers. Any producer who tries to develop more sustainable production techniques, yet links into existing marketing channels, is affected. The supermarket chains have such buying power that the continued existence of a local livestock market can literally depend on the presence of supermarket buyers to keep up the throughput. In Britain, it has been rumoured that buyers for the multiples are receiving under-counter payments to attend certain livestock markets. With little alternative but to sell to the multiples, and no bargaining power, British livestock farmers have been forced to accept a six-week delay in settling their bills — a form of free credit which they cannot afford.[16] Yet, as the supermarket chains achieve more power and success, their operations are spreading southwards. Southern Europe, with its more direct marketing channels has not yet been "modernized"; but giant retailing firms are moving in.

---

## Rocking the Boat

Mark Purdey, a small dairy farmer in the south-west of England, has been one of the few producers to have taken on the battle over the use of organo-phosphorous compounds in agriculture. He believes that organo-phosphates pose a threat to those working with them, to the animals that come into contact with them, and to consumers who eat products containing their residues.

In 1984 some of Purdey's young stock were away grazing in another area and as a result he was required by the Ministry of Agriculture, Fisheries and Food (MAFF) to treat them with organo-phosphorous warble dressings under "the Warble Order" of 1982. (In areas where warble flies have not been eradicated it is compulsory to treat animals on a preventative basis, even if they have not been infected by warble flies.) Purdey refused to treat his pedigree jersey cattle with organo-phosphates, and in 1985 was threatened by MAFF with prosecution.

In a letter to the organic publication New Farmer and Grower, Purdey outlined the reasoning behind his objections: "Having farmed for 10 years under viable organic husbandry systems, the organo-phosphorous compulsion has somewhat conflicted with my ethical stand, particularly as some produce from this farm is marketed to cancer and allergy clinics in London. I have always achieved 100%

---

warble eradication in our cattle using the prior 'approved' organic Derris compound, when there has been an outbreak in the past.

"Whilst in total agreement with MAFF over the need to eradicate the Warble Fly, it having a seemingly futile role in the ecosystem, I feel 'Derris' must remain as a legal alternative to the 90% effective organo-phosphorous compounds. Ironically MAFF eradicated Warble using Derris in trials in the Isle of Wight and the Isle of Man earlier this century, not to mention the total extermination in Scandinavia and Cyprus. I have offered the Ministry the full right to inspect our cattle during 'Derris' treatment operations in April if required, as a token of sincere co-operation and evidence. This has not been accepted.

"Our chief concern over the organo-phosphorous compounds lies in the legal limit of a mere six hours before the milk can be marketed after treatment. Surely if this esther of phosphoric acid circulates the blood system and couples with body fat, it will also couple to form the phospho-lipid fraction of milk, which is notably high in our Jersey cattle. ADAS and Central Veterinary Laboratories at Weybridge, Surrey have informed me that no tests on milk contamination from organo-phosphorous compounds have been carried out by them, but only by a commercial body that markets these products. I have been unable to acquire these results."

In 1985, with the backing of the organic movement, Purdey went to court over the issue. The basis of his case was that the Warble Fly Order is an instrument of the Animal Diseases Act which allows the compulsory use of a vaccine or serum only. As the warble dressing is neither vaccine nor serum, Purdey argued it was illegal to enforce its usage.

Although the case did not result in total victory for the organic movement, it did result in a defeat of MAFF's position that it had the right to enforce the use of organo-phosphates. Purdey was offered the alternative of treating some of his non-milking heifers with Ivomectin — a powerful insecticide — which he accepted. In general, the use of either organo-phosphorous dressings or powerful insecticides would mean a loss of organic status, so the solution was not totally satisfactory for other organic producers. Nevertheless, the case did demonstrate the neurological dangers of organo-phosphorous chemicals to consumers, the farmer operators, and treated livestock; and it acted as a focal case for many isolated victims to link up with each other and strengthen their stand. A year later the warblecide,

Fenthion, had its withdrawal period extended by twenty times — from 6 hours to 5 days.

After the dispute with MAFF, Purdey continued to voice his objections to the widespread use of organo-phosphorous compounds in agriculture, horticulture, forestry and industry. In 1987, he submitted evidence to the House of Commons agriculture select committee on links between these chemicals and increasing susceptibility to neurological, psychiatric and auto immune disorders such as multiple sclerosis, motor neurone disease, dementia, schizophrenia and "cot death" syndrome.

In the same year, MAFF cancelled Purdey's registration as a dairy farmer on the grounds that, on several visits, Ministry inspectors had found his herd of 70 Jersey cows to be unclean. Purdey maintained that his farm was in the cleanest state it had ever been and that if his licence was being revoked fairly, then the Ministry would have to close down 90% of all dairy farmers in the country. Purdey claimed that the Ministry's action was part of the sustained and systematic harassment from MAFF which had resulted from the publicising of his views about pesticides. According to the *Guardian*, "A Ministry spokeswoman said: 'Mr Purdey's claim that he has been harassed is completely without foundation'. She admitted, however, that the Milk Marketing Board, which repeatedly tested Mr Purdey's milk found it hygienically acceptable." It was not until the BBC came to Purdey's farm to make a film about pesticides that MAFF changed its mind and restored his licence.

After the court case with MAFF, Purdey moved to a new farm in Devon then to Wales and finally to Somerset to make a fresh start. As a small dairy farmer, working to self-imposed organic standards, Purdey and his family were just managing to make a living. Towards the end of 1990 Express Dairies decided to start retailing organic milk, and to Purdey's delight they offered to buy his milk at a premium.

Then, in December 1990, over the Christmas period, the Milk Marketing Board (MMB) alleged that Purdey's milk was "tainted" and refused to pick it up. Four days' supply had to be thrown away. Between Christmas and the New Year they picked up the milk as normal, but after the New Year again alleged "taint" and refused to take it. Allerted by the MMB and claiming "an emergency breakdown in hygiene", a MAFF Inspector made a surprise visit to Purdey's farm (usually visits are announced well in advance). The Inspector claimed to have found dung on the flanks, tails and udders of the cows and stale milk on the milk tank.

Purdey maintained that the Inspector arrived in the morning, before his normal "hot wash" routine had been carried out, and that housing animals on straw, instead of keeping them corralled in pens, is inclined to make them look messier. The real surprise was that a MAFF Inspector should have suspected a breakdown in hygiene. The alleged taint was thought by the MMB to have been caused by the cows being fed something like apples, which would have given the milk an "off taste"; it was not a matter of hygiene. Purdey's milk was at the time achieving the best "A band" assessment from the MMB for its quality.

By January 1991 the situation had begun to snowball. MAFF announced its intention to revoke Purdey's licence unless the situation improved; the MMB again alleged that Purdey's milk was tainted; and Express Dairies were threatening to pull out of the contract to buy Purdey's milk. Each time the MMB refused to pick up the milk, Purdey was having to drive 12 miles to Taunton to get a sample analysed by the Public Analysts. On no occasion did the Public Analysts find any trace of taint, and armed with this evidence Purdey managed to persuade the MMB to pick up the milk. MAFF Inspectors, however, were still maintaining that Purdey's milking operation was unclean, and continued to do so until the *Guardian* ran an article on the case in February, whereupon Purdey's farm passed the inspection. In February, however, the MMB continued to allege taint (again unconfirmed by the Public Analysts) and Express Dairies pulled out of their contract to buy Purdey's milk. Subsequently the entire organic "collection round" was abandoned, and Purdey and the other organic milk producers had to revert to supplying the local dairy through the MMB.

As a small farmer, lacking capital, Purdey had only been able to afford to buy land without a farmhouse. He had been given permission to live in a caravan whilst building up the business, but when, in 1991, he applied for permission to convert one of his barns to a dwelling, the Parish Council refused to lend its support to his application. One of the reasons for withholding support was that Purdey was not a competent farmer, a view they backed up by referring to the fact that MAFF had tried to revoke his licence. Another reason for rejecting the application was that Purdey himself had been on television highlighting the plight of small farmers and emphasising that they were barely able to make a living. Despite a report from the Agricultural Development and Advisory Service confirming that Purdey's was a viable business, the

Parish Council thus took the view that Purdey could not make a living on his farm, and therefore should not be granted planning permission.

Without the backing of the planners and the Parish Council, Purdey was pessimistic about his chances of getting approval for his barn conversion. Again, however, timely intervention by the media appeared to change people's minds. In the Autumn of 1991, a researcher from the BBC started to research a programme on the possible victimisation of organic farmers in West Somerset by the planners, and shortly afterwards 100% of the Councillors voted for Purdey's barn conversion, ignoring the negative comments which had been made by the Planning Officers.

If Purdey had not been so adept at using the media in his struggles, it seems unlikely that he would still be farming.

# Chapter Six

# Mainstream Responses

As the problems generated by industrial agriculture and food production mount, so too does the public pressure for change. Initially, the reaction of those with most to lose was to downplay the evidence of environmental damage and dismiss the threat to food quality. Straight denial has now shifted to a grudging acceptance of the need for reform, not least because of the economic costs of maintaining present systems. Agricultural subsidies in the EC alone cost taxpayers £24.9 billion a year.[1]

Two major problems have been acknowledged: supply/demand imbalances; and environmental degradation:

*Surpluses*

Surpluses have been a growing problem in the EC since the early 1980s, and in the US for a much longer period. For the majority of policy-makers, surplus production is not of itself seen as a problem in that, in the agricultural sector, as in other sectors, increased output is usually equated with increased efficiency: rather the "problem" is seen to lie in increased output leading to food being produced at a cost which makes its sale on world markets impossible without an export subsidy. It is the cost of that export subsidy — rather than, say, the impact of dumping subsidised produce on world markets — which most preoccupies mainstream politicians.

Prior to the 1980s, when output was low, the cost to the taxpayer of price support within the EC was negligible. At that time, levies on imported food could be used to compensate for domestic price support. However, given the favourable conditions for growth in agricultural output, self-sufficiency increased, income from import levies decreased, the cost of the CAP escalated, and surpluses had either to be destroyed or dumped on world markets. In the US, surpluses have a longer history than in the EC and have not been directly associated with such high costs to the taxpayer or the consumer. In the main, US farm policy has sought to stabilise farm incomes and prices either by opening up new markets abroad, or by restricting supply. These measures have themselves proved problematic.

### Environmental Degradation

Soil erosion, nitrate pollution of groundwater, the damage done by pesticides to wildlife, and the loss of habitats to agriculture are all environmental issues that have now made their way onto the political agenda. Environmentalists have been, for many years, fighting a rearguard battle to protect "special areas" from wholesale degradation as a result of the narrow pursuit of increased agricultural efficiency. Although attempts to preserve these "oases" still continue, a number of environmental organisations have begun to realise that without fundamental reform of agricultural policy, the environment and the countryside will suffer further damage as a result of the industrialised approach to agriculture.

There is also recognition of the problems being caused by the decline in agricultural employment and the disintegration of rural communities, though for the most part these are seen as an inevitable consequence of progress and increasing efficiency. But little or no attention has been paid to the interrelated nature of the multiple problems now facing agriculture and food production, or to their underlying causes. The pressing issues of energy use, consumer and farmer control over the production process, food quality, social justice and the need to support local community structures, have been swept under the carpet. Instead, policy makers continue to treat the many problems in agriculture as if they were unrelated to the system which caused them. The accent is thus on "fine-tuning" the system, tacking on environmental legislation where appropriate, and taking fiscal and other measures to reduce output.

The result is that layer after layer of technical fixes have been applied ad hoc to a system that is fundamentally flawed. The major issues thus remain unaddressed, whilst those that are addressed have been tackled in ways which, in many instances, exacerbate the very problems they are intended to "solve". Meanwhile, the number of "losers" in the system continues to grow.

The following policies, variously intended to address the issues of surpluses, environmental degradation and declining food quality, are illustrative of the problem.

## Set Aside

One of the perceived solutions to the problems of surpluses, both in the US and the EC, has been the removal of land from production under set-aside schemes. Such schemes, however, create a number of their own problems.

First, the land which farmers take out of production tends to be that which is least productive, and thus the land which contributes least to the surplus problem. The removal of a certain percentage of land from production is therefore not equivalent to reducing production by that percentage.

Second, the American experience shows that the land most likely to be taken out of production is not necessarily the land which is most vulnerable to erosion, or the land which is most ecologically valuable. The conservation and environmental benefits of set-aside can therefore be minimal. Moreover, the short-term nature of set-aside provides little incentive or opportunity to undertake land management of a kind that would provide lasting benefits for wildlife or the environment.

Third, farmers tend to try and compensate for the loss of land by increasing the intensity of production on the land which remains under cultivation. The net effect is often an expensive scheme which does little to reduce the overall surplus problem and which exacerbates the environmental problems on the land which remains in cultivation.

## Reduction in Subsidies

As the costs of surplus dumping have spiralled, and world market prices have been driven down by the amounts of subsidised food being exported, pressure to decrease subsidies and price support has increased. The thinking is clear: price support has led to the production of mountains of unwanted food and to intensification on the farm; if price support is reduced, the result will be smaller surpluses and less intensive farming.

In fact this does not follow. In Europe, price support has been blamed for surplus production, but in pre-CAP times — and in other countries — holding back price rises to below the cost of inflation has led farmers to intensify production in order to maintain their incomes. The idea that "lower farm product prices would lead to lowered use of inputs, improving the outlook for pollution control and decreasing energy use"[2] is therefore both unrealistic and oversimplistic. The evidence suggests that, in the absence of any alternative form of farm support, falling prices are likely to lead to greater intensification in the short term. In the long term, the abandonment of price support might lead to a restructuring of the farming industry, such that extensive farming would be the norm; but this would be like the phoenix rising from the ashes. In the meantime, farmers, with their fixed capital costs, would be going down like ninepins, with a devastating knock-on effect for both the environment and rural communities.

Moreover, the assumption that because commodity prices fall for farmers, consumers would also benefit from an identical reduction in price, has to be questioned. The evidence of the 1980s, when prices in many countries fell dramatically for producers, yet prices for consumers did not fall, suggests that the intermediaries in the food chain have little intention of passing on the benefits of price reductions. The enormous savings to be made from abolishing farm support, so widely discussed by consumer organisations, need therefore to be questioned rather more seriously. Though unlimited provision of support for each unit of output produced may encourage intensification, mere abolition of support will not encourage the development of more sustainable systems of agriculture.

## Sites of Special Scientific Interest (SSSIs)

The peak of the "protecting special areas" approach was probably reached in Britain with the introduction of legislation for protecting Sites of Special Scientific Interest (SSSIs) under the *Wildlife and Countryside Act 1981*. This established the concept of paying farmers not to damage special areas. However, although large sums of money have been paid out in compensation to farmers, large numbers of sites have also been damaged. In 1989 alone, 44 SSSIs were so badly damaged that they could no longer be considered for special status.[3] That designation is no guarantee of protection was illustrated by a decision taken in 1991 by Dorset County Council to build houses on an area of heathland with SSSI status. The decision was only overturned at the last minute following widespread public protest and an appeal to the Minister for the Environment.[4]

Within a system geared to increasing production and development, any attempt to designate certain areas as "special", and then protect them from change, is not only expensive, but also a fruitless task. Once it has been established that it is the farmer's right to do what he or she likes with the land unless compensated, any measures to protect the environment become extremely costly. If farmers have to be paid each and every year not to damage certain sites, there are a limited number of sites which can be protected without the costs becoming prohibitive. In effect, "experts" have to make impossible choices about which are the most valuable sites to be saved, and the whole scheme becomes an ongoing drain on the taxpayer.

A particular flaw in this approach is that only those who threaten to destroy sites will be paid compenstion. Those who have unique and well-cared for sites, and who have every intention of protecting them are therefore not given taxpayers' money; while those who know how to work the system, or who genuinely intend to destroy valuable features on their farms can extract compensation. In this way, the system contains a built-in bias towards environmentally-destructive farming.

## Environmentally Sensitive Areas (ESAs)

ESAs are another reflection of the attempt to divide up the countryside into those bits which are valuable, and therefore worth saving, and those which are not. The first schemes were introduced in Britain in 1987, although the legislation has now been extended to all member states of the European Community. Within the ESAs, the aim is to ensure that farmers are able to resist pressures to intensify production in ways that would damage the landscape or reduce the wildlife variety. Participation in ESA schemes is voluntary, but for those farmers taking part, payments are made for managing the land in an agreed way — often using traditional farming methods. The hope is that by stabilizing farming practices, it will become possible to conserve the chosen areas, whilst ensuring that farmers can continue to make a living by farming them.[5]

The problem with ESAs is that by defining certain parts of the countryside as being worth preserving, it suggests that the other parts are not. As Richard Body says "To draw a line across any part of our countryside, decreeing that one side is environmentally sensitive and the other is not, is absurd."[6] Moreover, because the emphasis is on preserving the most threatened landscapes, ESAs are virtually all in areas marginal for intensive agricultural production, such as the Welsh Mountains, the Pennines and the Norfolk Broads. Although these areas do undoubtedly need saving from the pressure to intensify production, other areas, more central to intensive production, are in need of policies which will reverse the damage already done. These areas are not covered by any form of protection scheme. Yet it is in these areas where the land is most vividly demonstrating the signs of misuse.

## Nitrate Sensitive Areas (NSAs)

NSAs are not so much a positive protective measure, as an attempt to put a plaster on the gaping wounds already caused by industrial agriculture. According to the EC Drinking Water Directive, agreed by all member states of the EC in 1980 and brought into force in 1985, nitrate concentrations over 50mg per litre are judged to be unsafe. However, even after 1985 the British government was still questioning the figure, and allowing nitrate concentrations up to 80mg/l. Only when a Friends of the Earth report drew attention to the breach of the Directive in 1986, and the government was threatened with prosecution in the European Court in 1988, did nitrate levels start to be given serious consideration.[7] Even then it took two years to introduce a pilot scheme for water protection zones (or NSAs), and it seems likely that new preventative measures will not be introduced before the end of a five-year pilot study.

First drafts of the NSA regulations suggested that farming practices, such as ploughing and the applications of fertiliser or manure, would be so severely restricted that even organic methods would be prohibited. The designation of NSAs therefore promotes a continuation of an approach which divides land use into "agriculture" and "conservation", with NSAs being seen as largely unsuitable for "agriculture". The absurdity of this situation is that Nitrate Sensitive Areas are *sensitive* to bad farming practice, and are therefore an indicator of the more widespread damage that will be caused if industrial methods of agriculture are continued.

When a smoke alarm goes off, it is not sensible to turn all attention on the alarm, while leaving the fire to blaze away untouched.

## Extensification

"Extensification" schemes, where the intensity of production, rather than the amount of land being cultivated, is reduced are a more positive step in the right direction of a sustainable agriculture. There is, however, little practical experience of such schemes, which are only beginning to be taken seriously as surplus problems grow. Within the EC, extensification has been seen mainly as an option within livestock farming, and whilst reduction in stocking rates is an important part of developing more sustainable systems, it cannot of itself be seen as a complete solution. Unless a reduction in stocking levels is combined with incentives to return to a mixed farming system, a reasonable rate of return for the farmer, and more local processing and marketing, reduced throughput will merely drive farmers out of business and decrease employment opportunities in rural areas. Furthermore, if the health of the livestock is not improved, and feed additives and antibiotics are still used, consumer concerns about food quality will not be addressed. Similarly, there is no guarantee that a simple reduction in stocking density will bring about substantial improvements for wildlife or the environment, though less intensive farming practices are obviously a good starting point.

In more general terms, low input agriculture is the counterpart of extensification in the livestock sector, and as such it is being promoted by many in government and within the mainstream conservation movement as a solution to the problems of conventional farming. Whilst any efforts to reduce the use of farm chemicals and to integrate environmental concerns into farm practices are to be applauded, the concept has been severely criticised by many in the organic movement, including the Soil Association, for the following reasons:

'First, no-one has defined what 'low input' actually entails. In practice, if other examples of industrial 'greening' are anything to go by, it will mean the well-publicized elimination of some of the most hazardous practices without any fundamental changes to farm practices. These cosmetic changes are happening anyway, while new problems, such as the abuse of biotechnology, are starting to affect us. In part, low input farming is currently gaining support precisely because it has not been defined.

"Second, there is no way of knowing whether low input agriculture will work. Whilst some of the most excessive over-intensification of agriculture could be abandoned tomorrow with almost zero effect on output, it is a moot point whether farmers using a conventional (as opposed to an organic) system could reduce the intensity of farming as much as is currently being claimed."[8]

## Food Quality Issues

There are several aspects of food production that have developed into major causes of concern for consumers in the 1980s. One set of concerns revolves around the substances which are added to food, either deliberately or accidentally, in the growing, storage or processing stages. A second set of concerns is associated with the possibility of diseases or infections being passed on through contaminated food: for example, the salmonella, listeria and BSE (bovine spongiform encephalopathy) scares in Britain. Thirdly, there is concern over new technological developments such as BST (Bovine Somatotropin) and food irradiation. And, finally, there is more general concern about the quality of the overall diet — including the proportion of fat, sugar and salt consumed — both because of the way these substances are used in processed food, and because of consumer choice.

Pressure from consumers has increasingly forced governments to take these issues seriously, though in many cases the responses have been *ad hoc* and have been directed at papering over the cracks. With the exception of a few countries, such as Sweden, the Netherlands and Denmark, which have attempted to do something about health and food quality and have introduced policies to reduce pesticide use, the official reaction has been to do as little as possible about these issues, preferring to leave it up to consumer choice and the free market. Under pressure from consumer groups, legislation on labelling has been tightened up; in the EC, individual additives now have to be identified. There is, however, still no requirement to identify chemicals used in the growing process, and little urgency directed towards identifying and removing the most dangerous chemicals from the production process.

The concept of labelling, grudgingly accepted by legislators, has the distinct advantage (from the point of view of the food industry) of placing the onus on the consumer to avoid unwanted products, rather than requiring the producer or processor to raise their standards. This encouragement for consumers to take "responsibility" for the food they eat is a favoured tactic of government because it does not require officials to tackle problems within the production process. While it is, of course, desirable for consumers to take some responsibility for what they eat, on the whole they lack any significant power to demand good quality food. In the US, bacterial contamination of chickens results in the death of 2,000 people a year in addition to 4 million cases of illness. In one processing plant, 58 per cent of chickens were contaminated before they went into the chill tank, where further cross-contamination can occur.[9] In the light of the enormity of the problems caused by the industrial production of food, the official view that "people wanting to avoid salmonella poisoning should cook chicken thoroughly and avoid eating raw eggs" seems to be a totally inadequate response.

In general, problems in animal production are only addressed when they become a public relations problem. Food poisoning outbreaks are a case in point. During the 1980s, the number of food poisoning cases in Britain rose significantly, reaching 20,000 cases in 1987.[10] Of foods implicated in outbreaks, those of animal origin dominated the picture, with poultry being the biggest offender.[11] Little official action was taken to deal with the problem until the "salmonella in eggs row" hit the headlines at the end of 1988. Even then, at the production end of the process, the regulations introduced for testing eggs for salmonella hit the smallest producers hardest, driving many small free range egg producers out of business. At no point was official consideration given to breaking the cycle of food contamination by halting the use of unnatural and unsuitable forms of protein in the food fed to chickens. Under organic standards, the use of animal protein in feed is banned; but animal protein was only removed from "conventional" cattle feed after the BSE problem reached epidemic proportions.

Many governments are now looking to technology to resolve the problems caused by intensification. A case in point is the selling of food irradiation as a "solution" to the problem of bacterial contamination in food. It is a response that typifies official attitudes to problem solving in general: rather than attack the problem at source, a new technology is introduced which demands minimum change to the status quo but which invariably creates problems of its own. Food irradiation involves exposing food to ionizing radiation at doses high enough to kill the bacteria responsible for food poisoning. The practice is already permitted in the USA and most EC countries, but is not widely used, mainly due to active consumer pressure. Irradiation causes foods to undergo chemical change, producing residues known as "radiolytic products", many of which are suspected carcinogens, mutagens and teratogens.[12] Bacterial contamination in foods may also be masked through irradiation, the bacteria that cause the food to smell (and thus deter humans from eating it) being killed. Consumers may thus be unaware that they are eating rotten food. Irradiation also causes a loss of vitamins in foods.

## Chapter Seven

# The Real Agenda: GATT and Biotechnology

The piecemeal approach of governments to the problems of industrial agriculture reflects a reluctance to address the deeper structural issues at stake. Explicitly or implicitly, large farming interests and the agrochemical industry are looking towards the development of a "two-track" agricultural system in Europe and elsewhere, with large farmers producing the bulk of the food, using industrial methods and making their way, by and large, in the open market, and smaller producers kept in farming through environmental and social grants.

In Europe, the trend towards "two-track" agriculture will be greatly accelerated by the removal of trade barriers, as intended, through the implementation of a single European market in 1992. As a recent report commissioned by the European Commission itself notes:

"The development of the Internal Market is likely to give rise to structural changes in agriculture . . . In certain areas, there may well be considerable 'industrialisation' of agriculture, in the form of vertical integration by food processing companies taking over the food production stage. This process will be facilitated by the removal of restrictions on capital movements which will accompany the completion of the Internal Market. A further impetus for structural change may arise from transfers of the production quotas which under the Common Agricultural Policy limit certain forms of agricultural output. At present quotas are allocated to specific land on the basis of the production level in a reference year. However if, in keeping with a market-led Community, quotas cease to be linked to specific land, transfers would be possible both within countries and across national boundaries. This could increase concentration of production in areas of greatest profitability. An increased market orientation, coupled with easing of market entry through the unrestricted movement of capital throughout the Community may give rise to a 'two-track' agricultural structure, increasing the dichotomy between 'agro-industrial' enterprises and less productive farms on the margins of profitability."[1]

## GATT

The agenda of the agro-industrial sector is now clear. To promote its interests — and in particular to allow the full development of biotechnology, which the industry sees as the key to its success in the future — an aggressive campaign has been launched to reduce the obstacles to further industrialisation and to further corporate control of food production. The immediate battle-ground is the Uruguay Round of the General Agreement on Tariffs and Trade (GATT), where new ground rules for international trade are currently being negotiated.

A prime aim of the GATT negotiations is to remove barriers to free trade in agricultural commodities. Whilst few doubt that the current system of subsidies is in need of radical reform, the proposals currently under discussion within GATT, if implemented, would *inter alia*:

- Drive the mass of small farmers out of business;

- Concentrate control of markets and inputs still further in the hands of the multinationals; and

- Remove the setting of safety limits for pesticides from national governments and place them in the hands of an unelected body.

The discussions, during the Uruguay round of the GATT, about the removal of agricultural subsidies have caused major problems between the US, the EC, and the group of countries known as the Cairns group. These disagreements have contributed to the delay in completing the round, with the EC in particular being reluctant to agree to large cuts in farm support.

Under pressure to produce a successful outcome to the Uruguay round, countries such as Germany and France have come under great pressure to give in and move towards acceptance of the free-traders dream of removing most or all agricultural subsidies within the coming decade. By the end of 1991, the GATT talks had officially broken down, and the GATT Director-General, Arthur Dunkel, announced a new package to reduce domestic farm subsidies, tariffs, quotas, and export aid.[2] To conform with this the EC's own reform of its CAP was also working on the basis of phasing out price support.

The removal of all barriers to trade is not in the interests of ordinary family farmers, nor in the interests of the development of environmentally friendly or sustainable agricultural practices. The removal of all forms of protection and price support is likely to bankrupt millions of small farmers, with devastating social and environmental consequences. It is no surprise that the bulk of American farmers, Japanese farmers, and European farmers are opposed to the proposed GATT reforms. By contrast, the biggest, most heavily capitalised farms are well-placed to resist cuts in subsidies (and indeed in prices) both because of their substantial operating margins, and because of the rate of technology-related productivity gains they are able to achieve. Such farms will inevitably expand their holdings by buying up the land of displaced smaller farmers. The result: fewer farmers, more intensive agriculture and more surpluses.

If the development of a sustainable approach to agriculture is not only about the use of non-destructive farming methods, but also about reconnecting producers and consumers, reducing the links in the food chain, removing power from the multinationals, ensuring that all consumers can afford to eat a balanced, health promoting diet, and revitalising local communities, it is difficult to see how an increase in international trade in food can provide many benefits.

Globally, the advantages will accrue mainly not to producers or consumers, but to multinational companies and to all those who insert themselves between the producer and the consumer, leading to greater penetration of corporations in food production. For consumers and producers alike, the consequences will be severe. An increase in the amount of food being produced in one country, and transported vast distances to be consumed by people in another country, will erode still further the little control that consumers have over the way food is produced. They will be unable to tell whether the food they get has been produced at the expense of the soil and the environment, they will not know what pesticides have been used on crops and how the animals have been reared. The result will be an even greater reliance on the regulatory process — a process which is all too easily manipulated by powerful interest groups.

## Codex Alimentarius

In that respect, the proposals within GATT to "harmonise" international regulations governing food quality and the environment are of major concern. Under the proposals, the Rome-based Codex Alimentarius Commission, a joint body of the UN Food and Agriculture Organisation and the World Health Organisation, would be responsible for setting standards internationally. Control over food quality will thus be removed from national and regional governments and transferred to an unelected body, heavily dominated by industry interests. The US delegation to Codex, for example, includes representatives of Nestlé, Coca-Cola, Pepsi, the American Association of Cereal Chemists, Hershey Foods, Smith-Kline Beecham and other corporate interests. No consumer groups or environmental groups are represented.[3] The pesticide committee of Codex Alimentarius has 197 participants: of those who attended a meeting in April 1991, 50 were from agrochemical companies, 14 from food companies, seven had no named or professional designation (which may or may not mean that they were consultants for industry) and just two were consumer representatives.[4]

By comparison with existing national standards governing food quality in the North, the standards recommended by Codex are generally lax. One study by Greenpeace USA found that the US Environmental Protection Agency's standards for benomyl on carrots, for instance, was 25 times higher than that of Codex. For aldicarb on potatoes, it was 16 times tougher; for diazinon on potatoes, it was five times tougher. All told, Codex standards were lower than current US standards for at least eight major pesticides.[5] In Australia, a recent study revealed that out of 135 cases where Australian standards are at variance with international standards, harmonisation would result in a lowering of those standards in 121 cases.[6] Yet, under the new rules proposed under GATT, attempts to enforce domestic standards stricter than those recommended by Codex on pesticide residues on imported food could result in GATT-sanctioned retaliation or in the demand for compensation to exporting countries.[7] In effect, "harmonisation" would lead to a lowering of standards to the detriment of consumers and the benefit of agro-industry.

## The Environment versus Free Trade

As a test case about the way in which conflicts between environmental and free trade issues would be resolved, the recent GATT ruling in a dispute between the US and Mexico over whether or not the US Marine Mammal Protection Act constituted a "barrier" to trade has sounded alarm bells for groups concerned with environmental protection. The Act was designed to protect dolphins from the worst excesses of tuna fishing in the Eastern Tropical Pacific. Dolphins and tuna are often found swimming together, and if the encirclement method is used to catch the tuna, the dolphins are also killed. An amendment to the MMPA in 1988 set a limit on the number of dolphins which could be killed by the US fishing fleet operating in the Eastern Tropical Pacific, the maximum in any year being 20,500. Countries whose fleets exceeded the US kill rate per ton of yellow-fin tuna would not be allowed to export their tuna to the US.[8]

In 1990, the Mexican fleet failed to meet the US standard, and Mexico responded to the embargo by filing a GATT challenge in February 1991. In August 1991, a GATT panel, consisting of three officials meeting behind closed doors, reached the decision that the US embargo represented a barrier to free trade. Since that time, the full GATT Council has twice deferred discussion of the panel's ruling.[9] The ruling has, nevertheless, united environmental groups in their concern over GATT. Barbara Britten, Washington Representative of the American Cetacean Society expressed her fears:

> "The impact of this decision is potentially devastating. This decision appears to say that no country may have a law to protect the environment or a species outside of its own geographic territory, including the global commons — the oceans and air — or the species inhabiting them if that law could also impact trade."[10]

John Fitzgerald, Counsel for Wildlife Policy of Defenders of Wildlife, voiced similar concerns:

> "This decision also brings into question a country's right to have environmental laws for the conservation of species and natural resources in other countries, such as the endangered species protections which prohibit trade in endangered species located in other countries. If adopted, this decision will conflict with and undermine numerous existing treaties and the environmental laws banning imports of African elephant ivory or halting the environmentally destructive practice of drift net fishing."[11]

Still more outspoken was Rodney E. Leonard, Executive Director of the Community Nutrition Institute:

> "It is outrageous. By eliminating the participation of all countries in worldwide environmental protections, the GATT leaves only itself as the protector of the global commons, which means no protection, because the GATT does not consider environment to be its business."[12]

## Biotechnology

As an integral part of their strategy to increase their control over the food production system, large multinationals are increasingly moving into the area of genetic engineering. Through careful public relations (not least the insistence on using the term "biotechnology" rather than the more accurate, but less natural-sounding, "genetic-engineering"), the industry has persuaded many that biotechnology offers the prospect of an environmentally-benign but highly productive and cost-effective agriculture. In particular, industry holds out the promise of a reduction in the use of chemicals through pest-resistant crops and crops that are able to fix their own nitrogen.

In fact, despite the claims of the industry, biotechnology is likely to lead agriculture further down the road of chemical dependency. It would be surprising if this were not the case. Corporations that have an interest in fertilisers and pesticides have moved into the seed industry, and now see genetic engineering as a logical extension of their business. Predictably, much of the work on crops involves making them more rather than less dependent on the use of chemicals. Thus, at a time when fertiliser use is causing environmental damage on a significant scale, research is being carried out into ways of making crops capable of absorbing greater quantities of synthetic fertilisers, and therefore, presumably, less able to function properly without them.[13] On the herbicide front, developments are even more worrying:

> "Worldwide, over 79 corporate/state research programmes are developing more than 23 herbicide-tolerant crop lines, including cotton, maize, corn, potato, rice, sorghum, soybean, wheat, tomato, alfalfa and sugar cane. The most likely result will be a greater entrenchment of the chemical approach, which in turn, will further increase soil and water pollution, pest resistance and chemical residues in food. In the process, natural ecological processes will be further distorted and diminishing biodiversity will worsen."[14]

That trend will be exacerbated by the growing concentration of the seed industry in the hands of a small number of large companies producing a limited number of crop varieties. The process of eliminating small companies and non-patented traditional varieties, which has already begun with the buying up of independent seed companies, will be pushed to its logical extreme by those interested in the commercial potential of genetic engineering. Yet, increased corporate control and decreased biodiversity are not part of a strategy for developing sustainable systems of agriculture. As Richard Hindmarsh, from Griffiths University in Australia, points out:

> "The ultimate danger of increased reliance on corporate r-DNA crop regimes is that eventually there will be few alternatives to genetically-engineered seed . . . Farmers who want to buy open-pollinated seed will find it increasingly hard to do so. Consequently, the current trend of farmers switching to ecological methods of farming, like permaculture, organic and biodynamic farming, could be seriously retarded."[15]

But, even if research into genetically-engineered organisms could be directed away from the narrow commercial interests of those who seek to increase dependence on chemical inputs, genetic engineering is not compatible with the development of sustainable systems. As Hindmarsh points out, genetic engineering is radically different from traditional plant breeding in that instead of operating at the level of the organism, it operates at the level of the cell "in order to produce altered, or novel, organisms that carry out "desired" or "programmed" functions, invariably to facilitate industrial production processes."[16] The result is that genetic material — either from another strain or species, or synthetically produced — can be transferred to totally unrelated species, so that they share each other's genetic material.

Although such techniques could enable genetic engineers to develop, for instance, a plant's resistance to attack from a certain kind of pest, in reality, the transfer of genetic material to unrelated species is likely to bring its own significant problems. Just as the widespread use of chemical pesticides has led to over 500 species of insects developing resistance to one or more chemical pesticides, so the use of transgenic biopesticides is likely to exert strong selection pressure for pests with a resistance to the natural biotoxins utilised.[17] Indeed, research in the laboratory already indicates that pests are capable of developing rapid resistance to genetically-engineered insecticidal crops, and it is probable that widespread resistance will develop soon after the crops begin to be grown on significant acreages.

Once pests have developed such resistance, the situation will be very much worse than it was before, in that crop varieties which traditionally have had good resistance to certain pests will no longer be immune from attack by the new strains of pests. Far from contributing to the development of sustainable systems of agriculture, the development of transgenic bio-pesticides threatens to undermine still further the possibility of developing any systems which are sustainable.

Added to the danger of developing pest resistance to natural toxins, is the fact that, once released into the environment, genetically-engineered organisms can no longer be controlled by scientists. Much of the concern surrounding the release of such organisms centres round the real danger that genetically-engineered plants might transfer their herbicide resistance to weeds; they might mutate and become toxic to beneficial insects instead of pests; and they might disrupt the natural balance of predators and polinators in a hundred and one unforeseen ways. As Paul Hatchwell notes in a recent study of the likely impact of genetic releases:

> "We clearly do not have the ability adequately to control the Pandora's Box of transgenic organisms about to be unleashed. The concept of

'genetic pollution' is not yet even recognized by society, yet in the Brave New World of genetic engineering it could be a more serious, though more insidious, threat to survival than current chemical and radiological pollution. Genetic engineering will not allow us the luxury of learning by our mistakes, as we have invariably done in the past."[18]

Indeed, as Hindmarsh concludes:

"The promises of the bioindustry that biotechnologies offer sustainability are naive, confused, flawed or just plain 'doublespeak'. When evaluated ecologically, they simply do not measure up. Instead, they threaten to undermine the prospects of attaining agricultural sustainability, for the overall risk with numerous large-scale releases of genetically-engineered organisms is to lessen natural species and genetic diversity, distort natural ecological processes, eventually disrupt ecosystems equilibrium and, possibly in the longer term, significantly impact biosphere equilibrium.'[19]

# Chapter Eight

# Movements for Change

There is nothing ordained about industrialised agriculture. Despite the pressure from governments, corporations, international bodies and consumers, there are farmers and growers who have defied conventional wisdom and successfully resisted the pressures to adopt intensive chemical farming. Over the years, they have resolutely ploughed their own furrow, building upon existing, and developing new, approaches for controlling pests and enhancing fertility without the use of synthetic chemicals; creating their own marketing networks; attempting, as far as possible, to evolve an agriculture that, in the words of Wendell Berry, "depletes neither the soil nor people."[1]

It has not been easy. Alternative, non-chemical, approaches are technically possible, but they operate within an economic and policy framework which is overtly hostile. Nevertheless, as Nicanor Perlas reports for the US:

"These farm rebels are succeeding and thriving. . . . There are more than 11 million organic gardeners who provide a fertile seedbed for the growth of sustainable agricultural consciousness among other consumers who may not be aware of the value of organic, bio-dynamic or pesticide-free food. In addition, there are more than 550 groups in the US working directly, even if uncoordinatedly, on diverse aspects of sustainable agriculture. Practically every state in the US has an active and dedicated organisation. These individuals and groups are involved in a vast range of activities including training and apprenticeship, research and demonstrations, conferences, publications, coalition building and policy work, certification, community building,

114

consultancy, managing resource libraries, conserving rare germplasm, supplying pest predators and other beneficial insects and large scale compost manufacturing. Sustainable agriculturalists have also established a national distribution network of dozens of companies and co-ops supplying over $170 million worth of organic food."[2]

What is happening in the US is also happening in other countries. But the trend is not all one way. Even as these alternative movements grow, industrialised agriculture is continuing to exert its influence. In Southern Europe, thousands of small traditional farmers are being swept off the land as industrial agriculture creeps southwards. In Britain, smaller family farms continue to go under on a daily basis, and even organic farmers are feeling the squeeze. Yet alternative approaches can be, and are being, developed.

## Movements for Change

Unlike industrialised agriculture, the alternative agriculture movement offers no single, all-encompassing "model" for farmers to follow: indeed, it is not even a single movement, but rather a spectrum of movements, the often subtle differences in their various approaches reflected by the terms they themselves use to describe the agriculture they practice — "alternative", "organic", "biological", "regenerative", "biodynamic", "ecological", "permaculture", "low external input", "fertility farming", "humus farming" and "holistic farming" being just a few of the many.

---

### Organic Agriculture

The key to successful organic systems lies in maintaining fertility through the cycling of nutrients. Crops which fix nitrogen are an essential part of organic rotations, and a balance is maintained between those crops which help to build fertility and those which exploit it. In Europe, most organic farms are mixed farms, and grass clover leys and livestock play an important part in building up fertility.

---

As livestock and arable enterprises are combined, both manures and straw play an important part in helping to close the nutrient cycle. Farmyard manure, produced particularly in the winter months when animals tend to be housed, is composted before being spread on the land. With an appropriate rotation, and careful timing of cultivations, organic systems can minimise unwanted losses from the system and achieve a good balance between the availability of and demand for nutrients.

Rotations also play an important part in preventing the build-up of pest, weed and disease problems. Just as crops which have the same nutrient requirements should not be grown in consecutive years, plants susceptible to the same pests and diseases are best separated both physically and temporally. Diversity within the system (different animals, different crops and different varieties) is one of the keys to preventing the presence of pests and diseases from building up to epidemic proportions. In livestock management, low stocking rates are considered essential; and the grazing of different species, with different associated parasites, either together or in rotation, is clearly effective. Experience with cattle also suggests that when animals of varying ages are grazed together, the likelihood of calves picking up parasites is reduced.

Pest and disease attack in arable and vegetable crops is reduced by the choice of resistant varieties, timing of sowing, and the breaking of pest and disease cycles through balanced rotations. It is important that the area sown to one crop should be restricted, as, in an ideal organic system, the ecosystem created within and around the crop encourages the predators of pests, which are an important part of natural checks and balances. Where appropriate, hedgerows and mixed planting breaks within fields are encouraged, as are companion planting and mixed cropping. Supplying the right balance of nutrients, in the right form, is also an essential part of enabling both plants and livestock to withstand attacks from pests and diseases. Weeds in organic systems are usually dealt with by mechanical rather than chemical means. The aim is not so much to eliminate weeds as to minimise the problems they cause. Effective rotational design is the first step in achieving this. Weed control can be achieved by "pre-seeding cultivations", such as ploughing and harrowing; but the choice of variety, sowing time and seed rate all have an effect on the extent to which weeds are able to compete with the growing crop.

## Organic Farming

In Europe and the US, organic or "biological" farming is the best known and most widely practised of the alternatives. At the farm level, organic farmers and growers seek, in the words of the International Federation of Organic Agriculture Movements, to:

- "Produce food of high nutritional quality in sufficient quantity;

- Work with natural systems rather than seeking to dominate them;

- Encourage and enhance biological cycles within the farming system, involving micro-organisms, soil flora and fauna, plants and animals;

- Maintain and increase the long-term fertility of soils;

- Use as far as possible renewable resources in locally organized agricultural systems;

- Work as much as possible with a closed system with regard to organic matter and nutrient elements;

- Give all livestock conditions of life that allow them to perform all aspects of their innate behaviour;

- Avoid all forms of pollution that may result from agricultural techniques;

- Maintain the genetic diversity of the agricultural system and its surroundings, including the protection of plant and wildlife habitats;

- Allow agricultural producers an adequate return and satisfaction from their work, including a safe working environment;

- Consider the wider social and ecological impact of the farming system."[3]

Specifically, organic farmers prohibit the use of agrochemical pesticides and avoid fertilisers in the form of soluble mineral salts. They encourage mixed farming and rotations which contribute to diversity; and avoid intensive livestock rearing methods, discouraging the use of routine preventative treatments for animal disease and prohibiting the use of artificial growth promoting substances.[4]

Since the early 1980s, a succession of reports (some official, some

# Kite's Nest — an Organic Farm in central England

Kite's Nest has been farmed organically since it was purchased by the Young family in 1980, but it is far from being a "conventionally run farm, without the chemicals". A 470 acre mixed farm on the northern slope of the Cotswolds, it is known principally for its beef herd and its wildlife.

On the best land, cereals are grown three years in seven, with a typical rotation being four years ryegrass/white clover ley, one year winter wheat, one year winter oats, one year spring barley, undersown with ryegrass/white clover ley. But much of the land is too steep for this and is down to permanent pasture. There are approximately 160 cattle on the farm (60 breeding cows) and the beef animals are slaughtered at two to two and a quarter years old. Throughout their lives they live in family groups, the calves are weaned naturally by the mother just before she is due to calve again, and whenever possible the cattle have the run of more than one field, so that they can make choices about what to graze and where to shelter.

The Youngs dislike the system of buying and selling through livestock markets, believing that it is unnecessarily stressful for the animals and a major potential source of livestock infection. In 1977, they took a decision to buy no more animals at auction and since then the herd has been closed, with all animals being bred on the farm, and inbreeding being prevented by the use of artificial insemination. In 1981, they established a farm butcher's shop, through which all animals have been sold since 1984. All animals reared on the farm are taken to a local abattoir, by appointment, where someone from the farm stays with them until they are killed. The meat is then taken back, butchered, and sold from the farm.

The system in operation at Kite's Nest puts emphasis on the health and happiness of the animals, the maintenance of rich and varied wildlife habitats, the closing of the fertility loop, and the production of healthy food. The Youngs are as proud of their wildflower bank and their bird population, as they are of their beef herd.

The stocking rate at Kite's Nest is low (1.2 hectares per livestock unit), and the Youngs could undoubtedly keep more animals using the same amount of land and labour. However, part of the reason for the low stocking rate is that no bought forage or concentrates are used, so they do not depend on "ghost acres" (see p.34–5). At Kite's Nest the cattle are reared and finished on grass, hay and silage, without being fed on concentrates. Despite the fact that no wormers have been used in the last 11 years, the animals are healthy and there is a total absence of lung or stomach worm problems. Overall vet bills are very low, though a vet is always called if needed. Furthermore, because the animals are content, they grow well without recourse to artificial drugs. The manure provided by the animals goes to fertilise the crops, and the straw from the crops provides bedding for the animals. To intensify either the cattle rearing or the cereal growing enterprises by using more outside inputs would be to destroy the balance within the system.

The customers who buy from the farm are equally committed to this kind of farming. They come, often from long distances, on a regular basis, to stock up with meat that tastes good and has been produced in a way which meets with their approval. Some used to be vegetarians, but feel that meat produced in this way is ethically acceptable. Kite's Nest Farm is up a long drive off a small country road; the shop does not get any passing traffic, nor is it advertised, yet through word of mouth, demand for the produce has grown significantly.

Like other British farms, however, Kite's Nest is now feeling the squeeze. Although both the cereals and the meat are sold at a premium because they are organic, this is a premium over and above the price for conventional produce, and reflects the increased costs of production. As the farm gate price for conventionally grown products falls, even organic farmers selling direct to the public are faced with the choice of keeping prices up (thereby effectively increasing the difference in price between their produce and conventionally grown produce) or allowing prices to fall. At the same time costs are going up. A nearby abattoir which they used to use closed a few years ago, which has resulted in a longer journey and increased slaughtering costs. The costs of butchering are going up, the cost of labour is going up, the cost of fuel and machinery is going up, the cost of borrowing remains high, but prices for farm products remain static or are falling. For those, like the Youngs, who believe intensification on the farm is inappropriate, the only option is to tighten their belts until it becomes impossible to tighten them any further, and they are driven off the land.

> At the time when there is so much talk of developing a sustainable agricultural system, it seems illogical to be forcing out of business those farmers who for years have been attempting to develop such systems.
>
> Kite's Nest does not fall within an Environmentally Sensitive Area, so there are no payments to be had for farming in an environmentally-friendly way. Although there are some special areas of grassland/wildflowers on the farm, payments would only be made to preserve them if they were under threat: the Youngs are not about to plough them up, so no payments are forthcoming. Even under the organic payment scheme which is likely to be introduced in Britain, Kite's Nest will lose out because it has already been converted to an organic system, and grants will only be paid to those converting to organic farming after the scheme comes into operation. Taxpayers' money, it seems, is not there to provide support for those genuinely trying to farm in a way that the public finds acceptable, it is only to be given to those who threaten to behave in a way that runs counter to the perceived public interest.
>
> As Richard Young says, "We farm this way because we believe it to be right. However, as we suffer more and more from the squeeze on farming, it is somewhat galling to know that if we had intensified when there were grants for doing so, and were now in the business of trying to undo that damage by extensifying, we would, in financial terms at least, have been considerably better off."

emanating from universities) have confirmed what "alternative" farmers on the ground already knew: namely that the agriculture which they practice is not only ecologically benign but capable of being economically attractive. As a 1980 report by the US Department of Agriculture (published but never implemented) concludes: "Contrary to popular belief, most organic farmers have not regressed to agriculture as it was practised in the 1930s . . . Most of the farmers with established organic systems reported that crop yields on a per-acre basis were comparable to those obtained on nearby chemical-intensive farms."[5] More recently, the US National Academy of Sciences came to a similar conclusion: "Farmers who adopt alternative farming systems often have productive and profitable operations, even though these farms usually function with relatively little help from commodity support programmes or extension."[6]

Other reports point to the reduced use of fossil fuels on organic farms, several studies suggesting that organic systems "require up to 60 per cent less fossil fuel energy per unit of food produced, even when the additional fuel used for weed control cultivation is taken into account."[7]

## Permaculture[8]

Whereas the roots of the organic movement stretch back to the early part of this century, the term "permaculture" was first coined by Bill Mollison in the 1970s. Thus although both movements share a concern to work with, rather than against nature, the permaculture philosophy is much more firmly focused on addressing the wider problems facing modern society. Advocates of permaculture systems have become as concerned about the design of cities, the use of water and energy, the exploitation of forests and the production of "wastes", as they have about the design of sustainable agricultural systems.

The permaculture philosophy centres round the ethical use of land. Taking design with nature as a touchstone, it enjoins the least change to obtain the greatest effect, employs biological synergy to limit entropy, and keeps close aim on net food and energy production, building of soil fertility and biomass, nutrient cycling and local economic self-reliance. If the discipline of applied ecology forms the basis of the technical side of permaculture, it also has a human and social side which advocates not only care for the earth, but also care for people. Many of those in the permaculture movement are openly critical of the emphasis in Northern societies placed upon appropriation, accumulation and excessive consumption. They see natural, diverse and productive systems as having been destroyed in favour of deadened industrial zones in which the production of single commodities has been pursued, ignoring natural limits. As Peter Bane, editor of the *Permaculture Activist*, expresses it:

> "By example, forests are our sources of stable climate, of pure water, of deepest mineral cycling, genetic preservation, medicine, fruit, and seed, and are the fount of our mental and spiritual well-being. They are not to be reduced to standing inventories of toilet paper and plyboard for the aggrandizement of a privileged class."[9]

In its broadest sense the permaculture philosophy is about assembling artificial biological communities which rapidly naturalise, becoming

# Permaculture in a Temperate Climate

Jerome Osentowski, a permaculture designer and teacher, operates Central Rocky Mountain Permaculture in Basalt, Colorado, USA, where he runs "Jerome's Organics", a market garden operation thriving in a cold mountain climate. His aim was to take a small, unproductive market garden, revamp it, make it larger and more productive, make it yield a living and to do all this with an integrated permaculture approach. In four years the market garden paid for all the facilities constructed on the site, including two greenhouses. The soil fertility was increased enormously. As with all good permaculture designs, it is still continuing to evolve.

The choice of land was incidental — it was the cheapest available in the area. Each year he would seed mulch another terrace, and the following year it would be planted, while the rock work for another terrace was started. This kind of gradual development is an important feature of permaculture systems. It avoids making mistakes by allowing time to look at the system and at the design, providing an opportunity to assess what is working and what the designer wants from the system. As Jerome needed an immediate income, annuals were planted and the soil fertility was built up. This provided a transitionary period of "rolling permaculture".

The design incorporates features of the native ecosystem. The idea of the green salads which Jerome markets came from several years of foraging for wild plants. It was commercialised by using cousins of these wild plants and developing a scheme for a very healthy salad mix. He also uses perennials and continues to use some wild plants in the mix.

The mixed green salad, as a marketing strategy, is both simple and diverse. By growing up to 25 different herbs and vegetables, the risk of a crop failing is dispersed. It is simple because it is a single market product, with one basic package, and all the crops can be picked and mixed together and marketed as one product.

Among the two dozen cultivated crops there is a wide range of needs and tolerances for climate. In the summer, basil is grown in the greenhouses where temperatures can go up to 32°C. In the spring, the greenhouse is used for bedding plants, giving them a head start and providing another market niche for that season. In the winter it is used for salad greens. Being flexible and diverse, it is possible to get the maximum use of the structures with the minimum input of energy. The gardens work the same way. The summer and spring gardens are planted with hardy salad greens. Most of the produce is hardy to −7°C. At 7,000ft, you have to have resilience through soil fertility and the genetic hardiness of the plants themselves. Each of the last four years, there has been a late June frost, one time reaching −6°C, but nothing was lost.

The garden system is further integrated with the greenhouses and the animals. The greenhouse system that has been developed is unique in that it heats the soil in the growing beds. Pipes carry warm ambient air from the greenhouse 3 feet down into the ground. Compost is used on the north wall of one greenhouse and on the west wall of the other — it heats directly through the wall and provides extra insulation. The chicken coop backs the west wall of one greenhouse, providing extra heat and carbon dioxide. From that chicken yard there is a very effective composting operation which uses a straw yard on a sloping hill. Large amounts of organic matter are placed at the top end. The chickens work the straw, rotten hay, or leaves, eat some of the weed seeds, shred it, manure it, and deposit it at the bottom of the slope, where it turns into high quality compost. This is then cycled back into the orchard and greenhouses. A lot of greenhouse residues are cycled in the same way. It all forms a tight fertility loop.

In addition to this, the chickens are used in a chicken tractor directly on the beds to recycle residues, control pests and manure the beds. In one season, seven chickens circulating on an entire terrace increased the soil depth by 4–7 inches. A pond is being developed with geese which free-range in the orchard — like the chickens a good source of fertiliser and pest control.

Other cultural practices include foliar feeding with seaweed fertilisers, biodynamic teas and a fish emulsion using waste fish from a local retailer. Sheet mulching and good water management have increased soil fertility resulting in extra hardy plants. The growing season is also extended by growing root vegetables which overwinter or are pulled and stored. In the autumn much of the garden is planted to spinach, which also winters over and becomes the first green in the salad mix, along with watercress in the spring.

In the beginning there were problems with pests, but as the soil has become more fertile, so the pest problem has decreased. Ladybirds were regularly released, until they started to breed on their own. A litter of cats is raised each year, and they control the mice in the greenhouses. A pest predator habitat has been created by planting *Umbelliferae*. Dill seeds are broadcast over the terraces in the autumn, and come up in the cracks between the rocks. The herb provides pest control and is also sold whilst not interfering with the main crop. Marigold and calendula are interplanted in the beds. Pest losses currently run at about 5%.

Marketing is across a broad spectrum — individuals, restaurants, supermarkets and farmer's markets. Produce accounts for about 65% of Jerome's income, and the nursery for another 15%. He gets a further 15% from educational work, and 5% from consulting.

The essence of any permaculture design is that it is constantly evolving. One of Jerome's goals is to become redundant. The evolution of the design is to phase out annuals and replace them with perennials. By converting part of the land to perennials: tree crops, fruits, berries, there will be a gradual shift in balance. Rather than getting locked into the market garden strategy, constantly putting more land into production, getting more markets, and employing more people, there is some latitude now to convert to a system that is highly productive, with less labour input.

*This box is an edited version of an interview by Peter Bane with Jerome Osentowski, published in* The Permaculture Activist, *May 1991. The text has been edited by George Sobol.*

self-maintaining and self-replicating. By encouraging a great diversity of different species, with different root and canopy levels, different nutrient demands, different heat-, drought-, and cold-tolerances, and different seasonal and cultivation requirements; and by selecting species which have at least three functions in the system, permaculture design aims to maximise the sum of yields and to support important functions with multiple elements, thus avoiding the catastrophic risks associated with monocultures, and at the same time producing more food, fuel, fibre and fodder than a single crop could ever produce from the same land. The development of such systems depends on an understanding of natural processes, and the use of time-tested traditional technologies and cultural adaptations, as well as empirical insights gained from science. With the emphasis on local production for local consumption, and maximizing output from diverse systems, permaculturists believe that existing wilderness and natural habitats should remain the domain of native plant/animal communities and those who have traditionally interacted with them.

At the level of practice, this broader philosophy translates into an emphasis on design within the system, and reliance on perennial crops. Permaculture, it is stressed, is not a technique: it is not about cabbages, livestock or compost. The individual elements of landscape, plants, animals, and structures, visible and invisible, are considered for the beneficial, or potentially harmful, connections between them, and how humans may place and manage those elements for mutual benefit, stability and the greatest sum of yields. Thus wastes from one part of the system become resources for another part, the different parts interacting and complementing each other in such a way that energy input is reduced and yields are increased.

In a permaculture system chicken, geese, sheep, pigs or other livestock may be run through orchards, where they control weeds and fertilise the trees. If legume trees or shrubs are interplanted, increasing nitrogen and providing leaf litter, the livestock may further harvest their seeds, inedible to humans, converting them to edible protein. Ponds can be used to check erosion caused by runoff, to retain water for dry periods, to modify microclimates, and to yield multiple species of fish, whilst also acting as a source of fertiliser and waste purification. Buildings are sited and designed so as to minimise energy use by capturing maximum solar gain in cold climates and employing natural ventilation in hot climates.

In moving away from a dependence on annual cropping patterns, permaculturists avoid ploughing and other soil cultivation practices which leave large areas of soil without cover and potentially open to erosion. In fact, permaculture systems aim to mimic natural ecosystems, not only having a diversity of species and varieties, but also a diversity of ages within the cropping system, and a diversity of heights. However, one of the key differences between organic farming and permaculture (which can, and often does, employ organic techniques) is that permaculture systems are more consciously designed to minimise the use of energy inputs. This is achieved through greater use of perennial crops (which also improves diversity), and through deliberately designing the farm system, including rotations and layout, so that energy requirements are minimised. As Peter Bane explains:

"The simplest answer to the problems of bringing energy expenditure back into line with energy production in agriculture is to grow the bulk of food near where people live, preferably within walking distance of the home, and to grow it with tree crops. This not only reduces transport but creates useful home-based employment, enhances human health through contact with nature, and improves freshness, and therefore quality of food, stimulates local area trading and cooperation, and increases decentralized political autonomy. It is a strategy appropriate to cities, towns and countryside alike, and one which should be undertaken immediately."[10]

## Permanent Pasture Systems[11]

Working in the same vein as the organic and permacultural movements, advocates of permanent pasture systems place a slightly different emphasis on the value of "traditional knowledge". Throughout Britain and the rest of Europe, it is argued, there remains, despite the chemical era, a reservoir of knowledge about extensive livestock rearing on permanent pasture land. These "traditional wisdoms", refined and passed on from one generation to another, are not taught in agricultural colleges, and are in danger of being lost as the chemical approach severs the links with the past.

Advocates of permanent pasture do not believe that ploughing up grassland as part of a rotational use of the land is to be recommended. It is when the soil is exposed, after ploughing, that the greatest amount of soil erosion takes place. Moreover, it is permanent pastures that provide the right conditions for the development of the biological activity necessary for healthy soil, vegetation and animals. In permanent pastures, the root system may extend to a depth of 20 feet, whereas in herbal leys the roots may go down only to 4 feet, and, in chemically-treated leys, to as little as six to twelve inches. It is the root system that provides the main mechanism for the recycling of minerals in the soil.

Diversity comes not from rotating one crop with another, but from the number of species present in the pasture. In permanent pastures that are well managed, the number of species present in the sward can average 60 or more in each field. The management is not routine mechanical maintenance, but an interaction between the animals grazed on the pastures and the number and variety of species present. Skilled management of pastures therefore requires knowledge of the interaction between the stock and the grass sward, rather than specific cultivation techniques. The type of knowledge required is gained by observation, and is passed on from generation to generation. In Britain, much, but not all, of this indigenous knowledge has been lost in the last 40 years, as chemical and technical fixes have replaced traditional practices.

Advocates of permanent pasture believe that during the period of intensive chemical farming, the soil has been severely eroded and degraded. The land's ability to recover is, however, remarkable, and the rehabilitation process requires not costly efforts to cultivate and reseed, but rather the adoption of techniques which allow natural processes to take over. Of prime importance in compacted and degraded soils is aeration, which allows seeds lying dormant in the soil to germinate and stimulates biological activity within the soil. As fertility is built up, earthworms take over the job of aerating the soil, more plant varieties grow, biological activity is stimulated and fertility is further enhanced. Such developments have been set in train by a number of different British farmers under quite different natural conditions.[12]

One of the main differences between permanent pasture systems and modern organic ones is the use of energy — both human and fossil fuel. Rotations in organic systems require considerable expenditure of energy in ploughing up leys, in moving animals, in producing and conserving animal feed, and in taking the feed to the animals. In contrast, advocates of permanent pasture are less involved in the manipulation of the natural environment, with the animals being encouraged to lead more independent lives.

A particular type of farming, known as foggage farming, eliminates altogether the need to conserve food during the summer for animals to eat during the winter. Under this system, blocks of pasture are shut up in succession over the summer, and are saved, without cutting, for the animals to graze over the winter. Other advocates of permanent pasture systems do make hay and silage in the summer and transport this in the summer months to store in the fields, so that animals can operate a self-feed system during the winter. In such permanent pasture systems, there is little use made of heavy machinery, and much less energy is expended in the process of animal keeping and rearing. Animal shelters are also kept simple, built of natural local materials, and are available to, rather than imposed on, animals. All these types of systems reduce the repetitive, routine tasks normally undertaken by humans when tending animals. They also reduce the use of fossil fuel energy.

Some of the most successful permanent pasture systems have been those that recognize the different uses of various types of land. Hill land, for instance, is ideal for giving animals a "summer break". It is cooler up on the hillsides and the animals have to move around to forage, in the process becoming fitter as they search for a varied diet. Sending animals up to the hills for a break in the summer can be beneficial both for pedigree animals, which go there for a short time, and for the hardier breeds which traditionally spend all summer on hill land. Resting the lowland pastures in summer and the hill grazing in winter is the traditional way of keeping the soil and pastures in good condition, and in the pre-chemical era was a part of good farming practice in many countries. It seems likely that there may also be a beneficial effect on the type of meat produced, as animals which are taking plenty of exercise are much less likely to run to fat than those intensively reared.

### Reintegrating Forests and Farms

Some groups, concerned about land-use rather than specifically about agriculture, have put forward proposals to alter the way land is used in their locality so that they provide for their own regional needs, rather than continuing to depend on other people's resources.

In Scotland, where forest cover is now down to 13 per cent, the vast majority of it consisting of ecologically unsound pine plantations, groups have come together to express the concern that their country has contributed to the global forest crisis through the historical deforestation of their own land; the limited and too frequently inappropriate subsequent reforestation; and the nature and extent of the demands placed by Scottish people on the forests of other countries.

The Scottish Forest Charter calls for a major new reforestation programme in Scotland "based on the principles of sustainable forest management as part of a comprehensive rural development strategy".

Such a land-use policy would aim to:

- Expand tree cover to an area at least twice its present size, approaching the global average of 31 per cent, including substantial increases in city forests and urban plantings of all sizes, in roadside plantings, lengths of hedgerows, shelterbelts, as well as small woodlands and large forests;

- Rebuild the fertility of eroded soils, the biodiversity and biomass of degraded erosystems for an eventual richer human inhabitation of the land;

- Conserve and recycle nutrients, protect soils and sustain plentiful and pure water sources.

Ultimately, it is the belief of the groups that drew up the Charter, that forests should

> "be managed for a wide variety of different products and goals — for renewable energy generation; for recreation; for carbon fixation; for wildlife conservation; for peace, beauty and wilderness values; and, as a priority, [to] help rebuild and diversify the local resource base of rural communities creating a forested country for people to enjoy living and working in."[13]

Similar demands are echoed by many groups around the world. In Australia, the The Men of the Trees have taken practical action to help plant trees on farmland, believing that trees, because of their "high shelter, deep roots and perennial green nature" will help to prevent the degradation of the soil. And further that "The survival of farmers and rural communities, which also includes the cities and urban communities, would depend upon rebuilding our soils and growing alternative crops and farm products."[14] The views and demands of such groups are not compatible with the division of land use into distinct categories — this bit being for housing, this for agriculture, and that bit for forestry. The demand is for a more flexible and integrated approach to land use; and for a land use which supplies local or regional needs.

## Community Supported Agriculture

Still other groups are attempting to develop more direct links between farmers and consumers and thus to regain control over the marketing of food from the food industry. Cutting down on the number of links in the food marketing chain is clearly in the financial interests of both consumers and farmers (in the US, for example, on average 60 per cent of the price that consumers pay for their food goes to intermediaries) and one response has been for farmers to form their own co-operatives to market their produce. Such co-operatives have enabled organic farmers to increase their bargaining power in the market place but have sometimes had the effect of further distancing producers from consumers, with the co-operative acting as an intermediary not between farmers and consumers, but between the farmers and supermarkets, in effect merely adding another link in the chain.

A more radical approach is being developed by the Community Supported Agriculture (CSA) movement in Europe and the US.[15] The unique feature about CSA initiatives is that they abandon traditional concepts of marketing. Instead of food production being the preoccupation of the farmer alone, the community (or a specific group of people from one local area) agrees to share the risks and responsibilities. In most instances, a detailed budget for the farm is drawn up on an annual basis, which includes wages for those working on the land, and then the costs are shared by the community which the farm will support. Sometimes this is done on the basis of pledges made at a meeting at the beginning of the season, the amount pledged varying according to the ability to pay.[16] One of the advantages for farmers of this system is that they start to get paid as soon as the crops are planted, rather than having to wait until crops are harvested before they receive any return.

Once the costs have been agreed, and produce becomes available, families get either a share of the produce, or take according to need (depending on the farm and what has been agreed). In the case of the Hudson–Mohawk community farm, some 20 miles north of Albany in New York State, for example, a single "share", costing $340 a year, provided enough vegetables to make four days' worth of meals a week.[17] Should a crop fail, however, then the 100 shareholders in the farm would bear the loss: indeed, it is central to the philosophy of the community-supported farm movement that shareholders should share the risks that most farmers have to take alone.[18] In 1986, when a thunderstorm over Indian Line Farm produced eight inches of rain in three hours, the winter storage/baking squash crop was badly affected. The shareholders experienced a loss of approximately

$35 each, but under a conventional system the farm family would have lost $3,500, which might well have left them in serious financial trouble.[19]

Because farmers know that their income is guaranteed and are growing produce for people and not for the market, they tend to grow a much wider variety of produce, and aim to provide what people want, instead of concentrating on the crops that give the highest returns. This diversity of crops within the farm creates conditions which are favourable for companion planting, and encourages the kind of integrated cropping practices which make crop failures less likely. The active involvement of shareholders in farm work is encouraged, a principal aim of the movement being to "reconnect" those whose primary activities lie outside farming with the land. This building up of a community, reconnected with the vagaries of nature, also means that other related issues — such as land ownership, conservation, recycling, and use of natural resources — become topics that are considered and discussed.[20]

In Europe, different forms of community supported agriculture have been

---

## Buschberghof — a Community Supported farm in Northern Germany

In 1969, a non-profit making organisation was formed and took over the land and buildings of two farms which had been run privately. Using bio-dynamic methods, the individual character and balance of the farm was developed, with improvements being made to both the soil and pasture. The philosophy behind the approach adopted on the farm was to eliminate personal profit as the major motive, and to use the land instead in order to provide a healthy living base for people, animals and plants. Milling and baking were carried out on the farm, and a milk processing unit was also developed. Produce was sold to customers through a farm shop, to shops in Hamburg and to the bio-dynamic distribution centre, also based in Hamburg.

Four years ago a decision was taken to change over to a community supported agriculture system. The idea was to involve people in the process of farming and in responsibility for the land. They believed not only that the land should be for general public use, but also that it should be the responsibility of all people, who should become aware that their habits of eating and living determine how the land is used.

In 1991 the farming responsibility was shared among four people (one couple and two single). There was one employee and five students who came to learn bio-dynamic farming and were paid pocket money in addition to their keep. The farmers have the responsibility of working out what it will cost to run the farm in the coming year, and the budget is sent out to participating households. Each household sends a proposal about the size of its contribution to the treasurer (a non-farmer), and if there is a shortfall the situation is discussed.

In Germany, a quarter of a hectare of usable land is available per person. The farm is 85 hectares, and it was therefore worked out that it should be able to support 288 people, or about 80 households. This it now does. Livestock on the farm includes Angler cows, pigs, sheep and chickens. On the 43 ha of arable land they grow wheat and rye for bread, barley and oats for feed, buckwheat, potatoes, and a wide variety of vegetables and herbs.

The 80 families are divided into nine different groups according to geographical area. Each group orders and collects its dairy produce from the farm independently, with each household providing its own clean utensils which are then filled by farm staff. The vegetables are distributed by a member of the community to every group, which then takes responsibility for delivering the produce to its members. The bread is baked weekly and is ordered and delivered with the vegetables.

The livestock is slaughtered by a local butcher outside the community, and is then collected and distributed. Roughly 30 pigs, 8 bullocks and 8 lambs are slaughtered each year. This provides those who want to, an opportunity to eat meat once or twice a week.

It is, however, the social aspect of the farm community which is radically different. In order to organise the distribution and understand the needs and wishes of families, it is essential to hold regular monthly meetings at which each group must be represented by at least one member. Thus, every group is kept informed. Some groups elect a representative every year for this purpose. At these meetings, there is a discussion about general farming issues, specific problems or new projects on the farm. The members have the opportunity to raise their own questions, for example, does there need to be so much salt in the cheese, or why are there no tomatoes in June when they are available in all the markets? These meetings give members an opportunity to keep in touch, and provide a minimum of information, though they are not enough to create a deeper understanding about farming processes among the members of the community.

This kind of understanding is increased by holding farm walks on some Sunday mornings during the spring and summer, whilst crops are growing. On these occasions, whole families walk through the fields, and later in the day discuss one particular topic, such as specific crops, the cattle, or one of the other enterprises. Some community members also come to work on the farm, which is the best way to understand the farming system. Some come regularly every week or so for several weeks during the summer. Working weekends are also organised to cope with certain labour intensive operations.

This kind of shared experience is more difficult to organise than a distribution system. Several years of working together are required before mutual trust is established. At first people and families do not know each other and do not share the same interests. Some join the community because of concern for the environment, others because they appreciate fresh food of high quality, and a few may join for the excitement of sharing a new social circle.

As Christina Groh, one of the founders, says: "This farm is now an integral part of all of our lives. It exists not chiefly to provide us with a living, nor to earn us fame by dramatically changing the world, but to recreate a bond between ourselves and the land. Each person has to create his or her own individual bond both with the land and also with the other members of the community. Initially we did not realise how dramatically the farm would be affected by these new practices. Usually farming today is thought of as an economic activity aiming for profit. Our aim is to produce the greatest variety of crops adapted to the needs of our local community. This concept is in fact much closer to a healthy way of farming, because an ecologically sound system has to be based on diversity."

Other advantages of the system are that there is very little use of packaging, energy used in distribution is kept to a minimum, and, as cosmetic grading is avoided, there is little waste of good food. Farmers are released from the need to spend time trying to market produce during the growing season, and although time is spent in discussions and planning with the community, this is mainly during the winter when there is less pressure on time.

in existence, in Switzerland for example, for over 25 years and are also to be found in Germany (*see* Box on p. 131). In North America, community farms have been developing since 1985, with around 80 in existence in 1990, and nearly 150 by 1991. Robyn VanEn, who has given many talks on CSAs, says the concept "creates almost instant empowerment. People go home and join or start a project."[21] Trauger Groh, one of the pioneers of community-supported farming in the United States, has outlined some of the important aspects of community supported farms in a book called *Farms of Tomorrow*:

> "Some things are typical for all community supported farms. In all of them there is a strong dedication to quality; most of them are organic or biodynamic farms, most of them show great diversification, most are integrated farm organisms having their own livestock and thus their own source of manure, or they are aiming in this direction. At all of them, far more people are working regularly per 100 acres than in conventionally run farms; and generally there are just many more people around participating in all of the dimensions of agricultural life: working, relaxing, storing, shopping, celebrating. This human element is of enormous importance. It shows that these farms have something to offer beyond good food. They embody educational and cultural elements that draw the interest of many people. Besides clean, healthy, lifegiving food, and a strong contribution to an improved environment, the educational and cultural elements constitute the third great gift that farms of tomorrow have to offer."[22]

In Japan, very similar systems have developed since the 1970s, and now there are a variety of groups operating in different ways, all aiming to reconnect farmers with consumers, and concentrating on good quality food. The biggest of these groups, the Seikatsu club, has over 150,000 members, and operates as a form of buyers' co-op.[23] Other groups share a similar sense of purpose, but are organized in different ways (*see* Box below).

---

### Japanese Farmer-Consumer Co-partnerships

In Japan there are over 660 producer/consumer groups supplying over 11 million people with food.

---

134

The largest of these is a co-operative known as the Seikatsu Club. Started, in 1965, by a housewife who was concerned about rising food prices, it was officially founded as a co-operative in 1968. Within the 20 years to 1988 it has grown to represent 153,000 members, grouped into 25,000 "hans", in 10 prefectures.

The Seikatsu Club operates a unique system based on: a) advance orders; b) distribution and payment based on a "han" or group; and c) the concept of one product/one variety. Members form groups of six to thirteen families and put in a collective bulk order once a month. Milk is delivered twice a week; eggs, pork, processed foods and seasonings once a week; and other goods, including rice, once a month. The han is responsible for collecting orders and money, and for collecting and distributing food amongst the families. The system is simplified by the fact that only one size and variety of each commodity is available. For instance, only thick soy sauce in a one litre bottle is supplied. This not only streamlines production and distribution, but also enables special demands to be made of the producer — like leaving out preservatives.

Though originally concerned with price, respect for the environment is now a fundamental part of the Seikatsu Club, and no products are handled which are considered to be detrimental to the health of members or the environment. The Club has developed direct links with organic farmers, and members agree to overlook physical imperfections in the crop in return for asking farmers to use fewer chemicals. The Club believes that "housewives can begin to create a society that is harmonious with nature by taking action from the home".

In the 1970s, women from the co-operative began to notice that synthetic soap was causing skin problems within their families. They managed to persuade 60–70 per cent of members to switch to natural soap and took the fight to local government level to try and get legislation enacted to prevent the use of synthetic detergents. In some local assemblies they met with success, but in many they were defeated. This became the start of a more active role in politics for some of the women. Campaigning on the slogan "Political reform from the kitchen", the club succeeded in getting 33 members of the club elected at municipal level. "The success of our 'housewives' has attracted the attention of women all over the country. Historically isolated in the home, the club has given women a vehicle for political involvement".

Many of the other farmer–consumer co-partnerships also originated with housewives. One group, the Miyoshi Village Co-partnership, began with the initiative of a group of urban housewives, who after several study group sessions in 1973, travelled to a village several hours drive outside of Tokyo to persuade an entire community of farmers to convert to safer and more sustainable agricultural techniques. Through personal introductions and lengthy negotiations over proposals, they were able to convince 32 farming households to provide urban households (now nearly a thousand) with a regular supply of vegetables, fruits, poultry, eggs, and grains in a direct, coordinated exchange.

Other farmer–consumer co-partnerships have been instigated by the farmer. The "Wakabakai" or "Young Leaf Society" was started nearly 20 years ago when Mr Ohira, a farmer in Setagaya ward, decided to give up using agricultural chemicals because of serious health problems. At first a small group of housewives from his neighbourhood became interested in his produce, and then demand began to grow. When Mr Ohira could no longer meet the growing demand for organic produce, he invited other producers to join him. The Wakabakai partnership now involves eleven farmers from several surrounding prefectures, and nearly 400 consumer families in and around Tokyo.

"Consumers have joined the co-partnership for a variety of reasons; the aspects most highly valued are the safety of the foods and the reliability of the supply. They also speak of imagining the 'farmer's face on the vegetables', implying that they value personally knowing the farming families who have taken responsibility for raising their food.

Prices are arrived at through mutual consultation at an annual meeting between all farmers and consumers, and records show considerable price stability over the last several years. Price comparisons range from about 10 to 15 per cent above to sometimes at or below the market price for conventionally raised produce, and almost always well below the price for advertised organic produce."

*This box is based upon information from The Seikatsu Club Consumers' Co-operative, 2-26-17, Miyasaka, Setagaya-Ku, Tokyo, Japan and a leaflet produced by The Japan Organic Agriculture Research Association.*

Clearly, these initiatives are not just an alternative way of financing farming, but are based on a completely different approach to agriculture, the land and the relationship between farmers and consumers. In that respect, community-supported farms extend self-reliance in two important directions: firstly, by abandoning reliance on traditional marketing channels, they reduce the power of the food industry; and secondly, by providing their own financial resources, they reduce their dependence on government support and financial institutions. Moreover, the tying of production and consumption to a community level has the potential to create extra jobs in processing, local transport and retailing. These activities tend to put the heart back into a community, whereas the type of jobs which might be lost, such as long-distance lorry driving tend to take people and work out of the community.

Indeed, a revival of more extensive contact between producers and consumers, and a return to community-based activities, has much to offer:

- Consumers benefit from seeing what takes place on a farm and how food is produced;

- Local consumption of produce reduces energy use in transport, reduces the need for sophisticated packaging, and allows the use of varieties which do not travel well;

- Consumers get access to fresh food at reasonable prices, and the need to preserve food with chemicals or process it is reduced;

- Consumers buying direct from the farmer are much more likely to tolerate a lower degree of uniformity and cosmetic perfection. This reduces the number of unsaleable "outgrades" and therefore gives a higher return to the farmer, or a lower cost to the consumer — possibly both;

- Both parties also gain financially from cutting out intermediaries and reducing transport and marketing costs;

- Local marketing allows the consumer to regain a degree of control over what is grown and how it is grown. Feedback from consumers goes direct to the farmer instead of being channelled through a third party.

## Eco-villages

In some countries, particularly Sweden, the concept of redeveloping self-reliant communities has been taken even further than the CSA model. In these villages, the aim is not only to connect the village with a farm so that the inhabitants get a fresh supply of healthy food, but also to reduce waste and minimise the use of non-renewable energy. The houses within the village are designed with energy efficiency in mind, and wastes, including human wastes, are separated, with waste water being filtered, and solids being composted. Although not all eco-villages immediately achieve all their aims, the number of eco-village associations is growing rapidly in Sweden — from only a handful a few years ago, to about 200 in March 1991.[24]

In Denmark, schemes integrating environmental housing and food production are also being developed. In Copenhagen, an existing area of housing in one of the less affluent parts of the city is being redeveloped to meet higher environmental standards, with much lower energy usage. The project which is still in the early stages has active community involvement, rather than being imposed from outside, and includes plans for the community to grow much of their own food, both in the limited space available around the housing area, and in conjunction with a farmer outside Copenhagen.[25] Eco-villages are also being developed in Australia, where permaculturist concerns have expanded beyond food production and land rehabilitation, into the areas of environmental housing, community development and natural resource conservation.[26]

Other eco–village developments are being based on the pond-dyke system which has operated sustainably in China for over 450 years. Combining fish farming in ponds, with livestock rearing and small-scale cultivation, small units of land can be made extremely productive without the use of chemicals. Clusters of such farms not only provide an income for farm families from a relatively small area of land, but can also provide for their own energy requirements through the production of biogas, and recycle virtually all their own wastes. Experimental units are being developed in Denmark and in French Guyana.[27]

## Land Trusts

Land speculation, the loss of land to urban development and the trend towards increasing concentration of landholdings has led many groups to evolve new patterns of land-ownership. The US, for example, has a growing movement in which farmers or other land owners sell or place their land in "Land Trusts". Whoever farms the land is granted the long-term right to use it under whatever conditions are agreed by the trustees: the sale of the land, however, is forbidden. In effect, as Marty Strange of the Centre for Rural Affairs notes, "the fundamental character of family farm agriculture — owner-operatorship — is preserved, but what the farmer owns is not the land but the long-term right to use it."[28] Indeed, many of the CSAs in the US are run on land owned by land trusts.

Once considered outrageously radical, land trusts and similar forms of land ownership are now gaining support within conventional quarters. "In some urban states within the US", reports Strange, "legislatures have authorized the state to take what amounts to an ownership interest in farmland by purchasing the right to develop the land from the owner. The owner gets the cash, pays lower property taxes because he or she no longer owns all the rights to the land, and keeps the land as a farm base. The purpose is to preserve farmland by preventing non-farmers from buying it for condominiums, parking lots and hotels. A half dozen or so eastern states concerned with haphazard development and loss of open space have adopted such programmes in recent years."[29]

## Consumer and Environmental Groups

Beyond the farm, a host of groups have sprung up since the 1960s to highlight the damage to public health and the environment caused by pesticides and fertilisers, and to campaign for stricter standards or for outright bans on harmful agrochemicals. Movements have emerged to campaign on the issue of declining food quality and against the increasing corporate control of the food industry; whilst biotechnology, and the dangers associated with genetic engineering, have become a particular focus for concern.

In Britain, one of the key groups pushing the debate on food quality in the last decade has been the London Food Commission, which was set up in 1985 with funding from the Greater London Council. In 1990 it scaled down its activities and changed its name to the Food Commission. Its concerns have ranged from pesticide and hormone residues in food, to food additives and food labelling. Successful campaigns were fought over Bovine Somatotropin (BST) and food irradiation. In 1988, the London Food Commission launched a new Food Quality Charter, which focused on the need to improve food quality; to provide consumers with better access to information; to improve democracy in decision making; and to tighten regulations.[30]

Similar calls for reform of the economic and institutional framework in which decisions on agriculture and food production are taken have been made by a wide range of other campaign organisations. At a meeting of the Ecological Consumers Groups in Bonn in April 1990, for example, 36 European groups demanded:

- An end to the current system of subsidy and price support where these encourage ecologically-damaging systems of production and distribution;

- That before being cleared for use, all new products should undergo a full environmental audit and safety testing and should be subject to the criterion of whether or not there is a need for them;

- An immediate ban on chemicals that are "dangerous to human or environmental health", including the "Dirty Dozen" pesticides identified by the Pesticide Action Network;

- A European-wide labelling scheme to identify pesticides used in the growing or processing of food, and a labelling scheme for all products which have been produced by genetic-engineering;

- The "right for consumers to take legal action against companies and governments which violate public health and the environment";

- A Freedom of Information Act and the legally-enforceable right to all government information and company information that affects consumers, health and the environment.[31]

The groups later formalized themselves into the European Ecological Consumers Coordination and agreed to co-ordinate their efforts on a Europe-wide basis to campaign against genetic engineering, food irradiation and dangerous chemicals, and for improved consumer rights, tougher product liability laws and tighter labelling and policing of organic produce to combat fraud.

## New Alliances

Joint campaigns, such as that initiated by the European Ecological

140

Consumers Coordination, reflect a growing realization amongst many activists that real change to the system cannot be achieved by groups acting on their own. In the US, a number of environmental and animal welfare groups have come together, in the wake of the GATT tuna case (*see* p.109), to campaign against the lowering of standards in the interest of international trade. In Britain and across Europe, animal welfare, farming, environmental and consumer groups came together at the end of 1991 to pressure the EC to extend its ban on the use of BST in Europe.[32]

Although alliances working on single issue campaigns can be very effective in demanding particular actions or legislative changes, there is also a growing recognition of the need for broader alliances between and within movements on a longer-term basis. Such alliances enable groups to campaign together for broad changes in policy direction, rather than concentrating their efforts solely on specific issues.

In Britain, for example, an alliance of farming, consumer, organic, animal welfare, environmental and third world development groups have created an alliance — the Sustainable Agriculture, Food and Environment, or SAFE, Alliance — to campaign for a radical restructuring of current systems of farm support. SAFE argues that if the link between increased output and price support were broken the financial incentives to more intensive production would diminish. "If this were combined with payments for sustainable farming, farm viability could be maintained in a way which commands public support."[33]

According to SAFE's campaign statement:

"Agriculture is about more than simply producing food. It is a way of life and makes a vital contribution to the health of rural communities. The central objectives of a sound agricultural policy should be:

- An agriculture that is supportive of rural communities, that halts the decline in full-time farm employment and provides a stable livelihood for farmers and farm workers;

- An agriculture that does not jeopardize the health of those who work or live on the land or the consumer through the use of polluting or toxic production methods;

- An agriculture that is capable of flexible response to national food and nutrition goals designed to improve public health;

141

- An agriculture that produces affordable food, of high nutritional quality and that minimizes chemical and microbiological contaminants;

- An agriculture that does not lead to the reduction of soil fertility, which minimizes reliance on non-renewable resources and which is sustainable;

- An agriculture that both conserves and enhances the countryside, not only in its visual aspect but also in terms of its resources and wildlife;

- An agriculture that respects the welfare needs of farm animals;

- An agriculture that does not threaten the development and maintenance of food security and sustainable agriculture in other countries, especially those in the Third World."[34]

More specifically, SAFE seeks to switch farm support away from price support towards payments for environmentally enhancing farm management practices agreed on a whole farm basis. All the land on any one farm would be included in the scheme, and payments made would be tiered on an acreage basis. The effect of providing "tiered" support through whole farm management agreements would be "to put smaller family farms (the mainstay of many rural communities) back on a level playing-field with larger farms, and to remove the present in-built bias towards increased farm size."[35]

Such whole farm management payments, argues SAFE, would have the twin attraction of encouraging participating farmers to modify their production methods to take full account of environmental factors, while simultaneously rewarding farmers already practising environmentally-sensitive farming, such as organic farmers.

Broad based alliances, such as SAFE, are also to be found in Belgium, Germany, and France. Although these alliances do not necessarily advocate the same mechanisms for bringing about change, their aims are very similar.

## Chapter Nine

# New Paths

The preceding chapter is a far from exhaustive review of the many initiatives being taken to challenge the current status quo in agriculture and food production. Out of those initiatives have grown a number of demands. These include:

- A reconsideration of land ownership, and the rights that ownership confers;

- An end to the environmental destruction caused by the adoption of inappropriate, intensive agricultural methods;

- The reduction or abolition of the use of agro-chemicals in agriculture, and their replacement with more natural biological processes for building fertility, and coping with weed, pest and disease problems;

- Legislation to protect animals from abuse; and the promotion of farming systems which take account of animals physiological and behavioural needs;

- Stricter pollution and food safety standards to ensure against contamination of food, water and the general environment by industrial and agricultural chemicals and by genetically-engineered organisms;

- Public access to all information relevant to the safety and environmental impact of farm chemicals, food additives and food processing aids;

- More open and representative structures for decision making, to ensure that environmental, consumer, small farm, public health, and alternative agriculture groups have a say in policy development;

- Legislation which enshrines the right of national and regional governments to set their own standards for food quality; allowing them to impose import bans on foods that do not meet those standards, and to protect domestic agriculture against imports of cheap food from abroad;

- Government encouragement for trading patterns that strengthen local markets and foster direct marketing links between farmers and consumers;

- An end to export dumping and other national and international policies which make it difficult for countries in the South to develop their own policies for self-reliance and sustainable agriculture;

- A more cautious approach towards genetic engineering and other programmes which could result in farmers becoming more dependent on chemicals and multinational companies;

- The switching of research funds away from the industrialised, technical-fix approach, towards more genuinely sustainable options, which are less energy intensive, more environmentally friendly, and which encourage diversity and the production of good quality food.

## Action at Different Levels

Just as groups are addressing a wide diversity of issues, so they are operating at a number of different levels. Some are working at developing alternative agricultural systems, others are concerned with halting the worst abuses of current agricultural practice. Some groups seek to use the political and regulatory framework to address existing problems, others believe that radical change can best be achieved by developing a new framework.

No one group can campaign effectively on all these issues, and yet where groups are campaigning on different aspects of a complex problem, contradictions inevitably occur. For instance, an individual farmer's switch to environmentally friendly farming practice, if linked into existing systems of distribution and marketing, runs the risk of being undermined. He or she will be voluntarily internalizing environmental costs in a system which gives the competitive edge to those that treat environmental destruction as an externality. The farmer who rejects the use of chemicals to help with yield, timing and uniformity faces the problem not only of higher costs, but also of falling foul of regulations and grading standards. Without a direct means of communicating with the consuming public, or a radical shift in the social and economic framework, such farmers will continue to operate at a disadvantage.

However, at the other end of the spectrum, statutory measures designed to require those involved in food production and processing to meet higher standards can also create their own problems. Environmental protection measures, such as enforced use of slurry handling systems, hit small farmers harder than large ones, not because small farmers are the worst polluters, but because they can least afford the capital investment. Regulations in the US designed to raise standards in meat packing plants required the replacement of wood with stainless steel throughout the plant. The result was that most small-town slaughtering facilities were simply forced out of business, and the meat industry became even more centralised.[1]

## No Single Blueprint

Neither individual changes in farming practice, nor changes in regulations, can by themselves adequately address the problems associated with industrialised agriculture. Indeed, groups campaigning in isolation for specific changes run the risk of just tinkering with a system that is fundamentally flawed and of being co-opted by the very processes and interests that they are seeking to change. Without deeper changes in modern industrial society, it is all too easy for a few components from an alternative approach to be tacked onto the agro–industrial system, "greening" it round the edges, while changing none of the fundamentals.

Equally, attempting to straight-jacket groups into accepting a single vision of the future to be achieved through adopting an all-encompassing "Blueprint for Change" is both unrealistic and potentially self-defeating. Different histories, differing environments, differing social conditions and differing political structures create different mixes of problems, which demand a diversity of responses. We cannot, today, invent an agricultural system that will be hailed for all time in all places as appropriate and sustainable. We can attempt, however, to foster structures that will allow and encourage the development of systems that are more sustainable and more just, recognizing that the systems themselves will need to evolve with changing circumstances. As Mahatma Gandhi rightly said, "The road is the goal."

## The Issue of Power

Industrial agriculture denies both consumers and farmers control over the production process, over its effect on the environment, its effect on animals, its effect on food quality; and over food prices and returns to farmers. A few boardroom decisions in the seed companies owned by the multinationals can wipe out of existence traditional varieties which have been grown for generations. A GATT panel consisting of three people can make a decision that trade should not be interfered with by people trying to protect species outside their own country. The release of a genetically-engineered organism, created by one company, could wreak untold damage.

At issue is the question of power — of who controls the land, inputs, production, marketing, research, decision-making and policy, and with what aims and priorities in mind. What unites groups, from farmers to environmentalists, from consumers to animal welfare campaigners, is the demand that they should have a say — that their future should not be decided entirely by others, and particularly not by industry, whose sights are set on market share and profits.

In order to campaign for changes of a structural nature, it is vital that groups should come together to form alliances which cut across narrow sectoral boundaries, allowing campaigns to be fought on a broader front. In forming such alliances, differences between groups do not magically disappear: the amount of weighting to be given to environmental protection, animal welfare, food quality, price, the protection of local communities, and so on, will always be a matter for negotiation. Those that have begun to form such alliances, however, have come to recognize that though the differences between groups should not be underplayed, they are of less importance than their common commitment to change — and that emphasizing them only plays into the hands of those wielding power.

# References

## Summary

1. "Shares of UK Grocery Market, 1989", *Which Way to Health*, October 1990, p.170.
2. Jackson, W., Berry, W. and Colman, B. (eds) *Meeting the Expectations of the Land: Essays in Sustainable Agriculture and Stewardship*, North Point Press, San Francisco, 1984, p.x.

## Industrial Agriculture: Heading for Disaster

1. Strange, M., *Family Farming: A New Economic Vision*, University of Nebraska Press and Institute of Food and Development Policy, Lincoln, London, San Francisco, 1988, p.178.
2. National Academy of Sciences/National Research Council, *Alternative Agriculture*, National Academy Press, Washington DC, 1989, p.120.
3. Ministry of Agriculture, Fisheries and Food, Northern Ireland Office, Scottish Office and Welsh Office, *Farming U.K.*, HMSO, London, 1987.
4. Body, R., *Our Food, Our Land: Why contemporary farming practices must change*, Rider, London, 1991, p.114.
5. Sustainable Agriculture Food and Environment (SAFE) Alliance, press release 14/11/91.
6. Belden, J.N., *Dirt Rich, Dirt Poor: America's Food and Farm Crisis*, Routledge and Kegan Paul, New York and London, 1986, p.3.
7. Krebs, A.V., *The Corporate Reapers, the Book of Agribusiness*, Essential Books, Washington DC, forthcoming.
8. Davies, R., "Shock for Welsh as hill incomes plunge", *Farmers Weekly* 12 October 1990, p.15.
9. Body, op. cit. 4, p.85.
10. Lowe, P., Cox, G., MacEwen, M., O'Riordan, T. and Winter, M., *Countryside Conflicts: the politics of farming, forestry and conservation*, Gower, Aldershot, 1986, chapter 13.

REFERENCES

11. Countryside Commission, *Upland Land Use in England and Wales*, Countryside Commission, Cheltenham, 1978. Cited in Irvine, A.B., *Ecocentrism, Rural Resource Management and the British Uplands*, M.Sc. Thesis, Dept of Town and Country Planning, University of Newcastle Upon Tyne, December, 1990.

12. Irvine, A.B., *Ecocentrism, Rural Resource Management and the British Uplands*, M.Sc. Thesis, Dept of Town and Country Planning, University of Newcastle Upon Tyne, December, 1990.

13. Countryside Commission, op. cit. 11.

14. Norton-Taylor, R., *Whose Land is it Anyway?*, Turnstone Press, Wellingborough, 1982, pp.17–59.

15. Shoard, M., *This Land is Our Land*, Paladin, London, 1987, pp.97–103.

16. Norton-Taylor, op. cit. 14.

17. MacEwan, A. and MacEwan, M., *National Parks: Conservation or Cosmetics?*, Allen and Unwin, London, 1982.

18. Shoard, op. cit.15, p.489.

19. Sachs, C.E., *The Invisible Farmers: Women in Agricultural Production*, Rowman and Allanheld, USA, 1983, p.39.

20. Whatmore, S., *Farming Women: Gender, Work and Family Enterprise*, Macmillan, London, 1991, p.69.

21. British Population Census 1981, HMSO, London, 1982.

22. Gasson, R., "Roles of Women on Farms: A Pilot Study", *Journal of Agricultural Economics*, 32, pp.11–20.

23. Edwards, R., "Scotland: Behind the Scenery", *Social Work Today* 14 (27), 1983, pp.10–14: McLaughlin, B.R., "Rural Deprivation", *The Planner*, 67, 1981, pp.31–33: Newby, H., *A Green and Pleasant Land?*, Hutchinson, London, 1979.

24. Norton-Taylor, op. cit. 14.

25. MacEwan and MacEwan, op. cit. 17.

26. Personal communication from Isabel Bermejo of CODA (Coordinadora de Organizaciones de Defensa Ambiental), Spain.

27. Hunt, J., "2,500 producers suffer OP dip side effects" *Farmers Weekly* 14 December 1990, p.12.

28. Rose, C., "Pesticides: An industry out of control" in Goldsmith, E. and Hildyard, N. (eds), *Green Britain or Industrial Wasteland*, Polity Press, Cambridge, 1986, p.156.

29. The London Food Commission *Food adulteration and how to beat it*, Unwin, London, 1988, p.79.

30. Department of Environment statistics, 1988, quoted in Soil Association, *Guidelines for Conservation*, Soil Association, Bristol, February 1990, p.7.

31. Hawkes, N., "Anti-pest grass", *The Times* 25 February 1992.

32. Royal Society for Nature Conservation (RSNC) and the Wildlife Trusts Partnership, *Focus on Meadows*, RSNC, Lincoln, January 1991.
33. Irvine, A.B., op. cit. 11.
34. Ibid.
35. RSNC, op. cit. 32.
36. Ibid.
37. Department of Environment statistics, 1988, quoted in Soil Association, op. cit. 30.
38. Personal communication from Thymio Papayannis, Chair, MedWet CoG, 23 Voukourestiou Str., 10671 Athens, Greece.
39. Goldsmith, E. and Hildyard, N. (eds), *The Earth Report 2, monitoring the battle for the Environment*, Mitchell Beazley, London, 1990, p.167.
40. Goldsmith, E., Hildyard, N., McCully, P. and Bunyard, P., *5000 Days to Save the Planet*, Hamlyn, London, 1990, p.151.
41. Ibid, pp.116–127.
42. Brown, L.R. et al., *State of the World 1990*, Norton, New York and London, 1990, p.60. The figure is for soil loss in excess of new soil formation.
43. Body, op. cit. 4, p.14.
44. Ibid.
45. Ibid, p.23.
46. Belden, J.N., op. cit. 6, p.6.
47. The US Department of Agriculture classifies 7 per cent of agricultural land in North America as suffering severe erosion, its productive potential reduced by more than 50 per cent. A further 23 per cent suffered moderate erosion with a 10–50 per cent reduction in potential. See: USDA Economic Research Service, *World Agriculture Situation and Outlook Report*, Washington DC, 1989.
48. For a discussion of this see Lampkin, N., *Organic Farming*, Farming Press, Ipswich, 1990, pp.36–42.
49. Goldsmith, E., "Agroecosytems and their destruction", Draft manuscript, 1990.
50. Stokes, B., *Bread and Water: Growing Tomorrow's Food*, Unpublished manuscript, 1980, p.5.
51. Ibid, Sec. 4, p.2.
52. Goldsmith, E. et al, op. cit. 40, p.113.
53. Harle, N., "The Ecological Impact of Overdevelopment: A Case Study of the Limburg Borderlands", *The Ecologist* Vol. 20, No. 5, September/October 1990, pp. 182–189.
54. Zidek, T., "CSFR: New State, New Priorities", in *Signs of Hope*, Farmers' Link/Food Matters Worldwide, Norwich, 1991, p.22.
55. For a discussion of water shortages in the US and the politics of irrigation

agriculture, *see* Reisner, M., *Cadillac Desert: The American West and Its Disappearing Water*, Secker and Warburg, London, 1990.

56. "Advance Census Reports Show Irrigation Rebound", *Agricultural Outlook*, May 1989. Cited in Sandra Postel, "Saving Water for Agriculture" in Brown, L.R. et al., op. cit. 42, p.46.

57. Reisner, M., op. cit. 55, p.386.

58. World Resources Institute/International Institute for Environment and Development/United Nations Environment Programme, *World Resources 1988–89*, Basic Books, New York, 1989, p.135. *See also:* "Groundwater Ills: Many Diagnoses, Few Remedies", *Science*, Vol. 232, pp.1490–1493, 20 June 1986 and Office of Technology Assessment, *Protecting the Nation's Groundwater from Contamination*, Washington, 1984.

59. National Academy of Sciences/National Research Council, op. cit. 2, p.105. See also: US Department of Agriculture, *The Magnitude and Costs of Groundwater Contamination from Agricultural Chemicals — A National Perspective*, Staff Report AGES870318, Economic Research Service, Washington DC, 1987.

60. In 1986, the Iowa Department of Water, Air and Waste Management reported finding pesticides and other synthetic chemicals "in half of Iowa's city wells". *See:* "Groundwater Ills: Many Diagnoses, Few Remedies', *Science*, Vol. 232, pp.1490–1493, 20 June 1986.

61. Greenpeace New Zealand, *Ecological Agriculture in New Zealand: Greenpeace NZ submission to Ministry of Agriculture and Fisheries on MAF Policy Paper 106: Sustainable Agriculture, A Policy Proposal*, Greenpeace New Zealand, Auckland, July 1991.

62. Brown, P., "Water firms face criminal action over 'unfit' supplies" *The Guardian*, 18 July 1991.

63. World Resources Institute/International Institute for Environment and Development/United Nations Environment Programme, op. cit. 59, p.137.

64. Meybeck, M., Chapman, D., and Helmer R. (eds), *Global Freshwater Quality: A First Assessment*, World Health Organisation/United Nations Environment Programme, Blackwell, Oxford, 1989, p.133.

65. Lang, T., *Food Policy and the New Consumer — Some UK and European Experiences*, Australian Consumers' Association, Australia, 1990, p.3.

66. Hume Hall, R., "What's in a Pizza?", *The New Ecologist*, Vol. 9, No. 1, January/February, 1979, p.18.

67. Hume Hall, R., "Dangerous Practices in Food Technology", *The New Ecologist*, No. 1, January/February, 1978, p.28.

68. Lang, T., op. cit. 65, p.16.

69. Millstone, E., "Food Additives: What are we Really Eating?" in Goldsmith, E. and Hildyard, N. (eds), op. cit. 28.

70. London Food Commission, op. cit. 29, p.45.
71. For a full discussion, see London Food Commission, op. cit. 29, chapters 1 and 3.
72. Rose, C., op. cit. 28, p.143.
73. Briggs, S.A., "Silent Spring: The View from 1990", *The Ecologist*, Vol. 20. No. 2, March/April 1990, p.55.
74. National Academy of Sciences, *Toxicity Testing: Strategies to Determine Needs and Priorities*, National Academy of Sciences, Washington, 1984.
75. Briggs, S.A., op. cit. 73, p.56.
76. London Food Commission, op. cit. 29, p.98.
77. Ibid.
78. Goldsmith, E. et al., op. cit. 40.
79. Snell, P., "Pesticide Residues: The Scandal Continues", *The Ecologist*, Vol. 19, No. 3, 1989, p.95. *See also:* Ministry of Agriculture, Fisheries and Food, *Report of the Working Party on Pesticide Residues 1985–1988*, Food Surveillance Paper No. 25, HMSO, London, 1989.
80. Ibid.
81. Gips, T./International Alliance for Sustainable Agriculture, *Breaking the Pesticide Habitat: Alternatives to 12 Hazardous Pesticides*, International Organization of Consumers Unions, Penang, 1990, p.3.
82. Snell, P., op. cit. 79, p.95.
83. Goldsmith, J., *Intensive Farming, the CAP and GATT*, Caroline Walker Lecture, 16 October 1991, published privately, 1991.
84. The Animal Welfare Institute, *Factory Farming: The Experiment That Failed*, The Animal Welfare Institute, USA, 1987, p.7.
85. Erlichman, J., "Progress halves chickens' lifespan", *The Guardian*, 15 October 1991, p.4.
86. Ibid.
87. Long, A., "The Salmonella Epidemic", *The Ecologist*, Vol. 18, No. 6, November/December 1988, p.190.
88. Ibid, p.191.
89. Erlichman, J., *Gluttons for Punishment*, Penguin, Harmondsworth, 1986, Chapter 3.
90. "Senate Exposé: 400% increase in bacterial contamination of mass-produced chickens", draft of an article for The Animal Welfare Institute Quarterly, USA.
91. Ibid.
92. Ibid.
93. Epstein, S.S., "BST: The Public Health Hazards", *The Ecologist*, Vol. 19, No. 5, September/October 1989, pp.191–195.
94. De Kleine Aarde, "Dutch agriculture far from Sustainable", factsheet

12 April 1991.
95. Goldsmith and Hildyard, op. cit. 39, p.80.
96. Tadeu Caldas, in *Signs of Hope*, op. cit. 54, p.9.
97. Information provided by Bill Barclay, Pesticides Project, Greenpeace International, USA.
98. Ibid.
99. De Kleine Aarde, op. cit. 94.
100. Talk given by Rudolf Buntzel of the Protestant Farmers Association of Wurtemberg, at the Catholic Institute for International Relations seminar "The GATT, Agricultural Reform and the future of the Common Agriculture Policy", 11 October 1991.
101. Belden, J.N., op. cit. 6, p.7.
102. Ministry of Agriculture, Fisheries and Food et al., op. cit. 3, p.11.
103. Belden, op. cit. 6, p.6.
104. Coleman, A., "Is Planning Really Necessary?", The Geographical Journal, Vol. 142, part 3, November 1976.
105. Body, R., *Agriculture: The Triumph and The Shame*, Temple Smith, London, 1982, p.38.
106. Hall, C., Cleveland, C. and Kaufmann, R., *Energy and Resource Quality*, Wiley, New York, Chichester, 1986, pp.124–5.
107. Body, R., op. cit. 4, p.6.
108. Hall et al., op. cit. 105.
109. Ibid.
110. Belden op. cit. 5, p.6.
111. McCully, P., "The End of Industrialism", *The Ecologist*, Vol. 20, No. 5, September/October 1990.

## *Pushed onto the Treadmill*

1. *Hansard* 14 April 1991, HMSO, London, 1991.
2. *Hansard* 18 April 1991, HMSO, London, 1991.
3. Body, R., *Our Food, Our Land: Why contemporary farming practices must change*, Rider, London, 1991, p.96.
4. Ministry of Agriculture, Fisheries and Food, *Loaves and Fishes: an illustrated history of the Ministry of Agriculture, Fisheries and Food 1889–1989*, HMSO, London, 1989, p.34.
5. Ibid, p.49.
6. Lowe, P., Cox, G., MacEwen, M., O'Riordan, T. and Winter, M., *Countryside Conflicts: the politics of farming, forestry and conservation*, Gower, Aldershot, 1986, p.41.
7. Ibid.

8. Ibid, p.38.
9. Ibid, p.43.
10. Ibid.
11. Commission of the European Communities, *Communication of the Commission to the Council: The Development and Future of the CAP, Reflection Paper of the Commission*, COM (91) 100 Final, Brussels, 1 February 1991.
12. Shoard, M., *This Land is Our Land*, Paladin, London, 1987, p.145.
13. Personal communication from Simon Fairlie, November 1991.
14. Information Provided by Simone Caillot and translated into English by Simon Fairlie.
15. All the information on Spain provided by Isabel Bermejo of CODA (Coordinadora de Organizaciones de Defensa Ambiental), Spain and CEPA (Coordinora Extremena de Proteccion Ambiental).
16. National Academy of Sciences/National Research Council, *Alternative Agriculture*, National Academy Press, Washington DC, 1989, p.69.
17. Ibid, p.10.
18. Information provided by Mark Ritchie, Institute of Agriculture and Trade Policy, Minneapolis, USA, in response to first draft.
19. Krebs, A.V., *The Corporate Reapers, the Book of Agribusiness*, Essential Books, Washington DC, forthcoming.
20. National Academy of Sciences/National Research Council, op. cit. 16, p.73.
21. Ibid, p.77.
22. Ibid, p.76.
23. Ibid. pp.69 and 235.
24. Ibid, 235.

## *Caught on the Treadmill*

1. For an excellent treatment of this shift in bargaining power, see Strange, M., *Family Farming: A New Economic Vision*, University of Nebraska Press and Institute of Food and Development Policy, Lincoln, London, San Francisco, 1988.
2. Mooney, P. and Fowler, C., unpublished article submitted to *The Ecologist*. For excellent accounts of how large corporations have moved to take over small independent seed businesses, see Fowler, C. and Mooney, P., *Shattering: Food, politics and the loss of genetic diversity*, University of Arizona Press, 1990, pp.118–139 and Hobbelink, H., *Biotechnology and the Future of World Agriculture*, Zed Books, London, 1991.
3. Fowler and Mooney. Ibid, p.125.
4. Hobbelink, H., *Biotechnology and the Future of World Agriculture*, Zed Books, London, 1991, p.45. See also: *Environment Digest* No. 2.

5. Ibid, p.45.
6. Fowler and Mooney, op. cit. pp.123–4.
7. Ibid, p.124.
8. Ibid, p.133.
9. Ibid, p.133.
10. Goering, P., Norberg-Hodge, H., Page, J., Agriculture: Making the Connections, Draft, International Society for Ecology and Culture, 1991, p.1.
11. Hobbelink, H., op. cit. 4, Table 5.1, pp.55–58.
12. Fowler, C. and Mooney, P., op. cit. 2, p.132.
13. Body, R., *Our Food, Our Land: Why contemporary farming practices must change*, Rider, 1991, p.29.
14. Strange, M., op. cit. 1, p.114.
15. National Academy of Sciences/National Research Council, *Alternative Agriculture*, National Academy Press, Washington, DC, 1989, p.38.
16. Belden, J.N., *Dirt Rich, Dirt Poor: America's Food and Farm Crisis*, Routledge and Kegan Paul, New York and London, 1986, p.33.
17. Ibid, p.34.
18. National Academy of Sciences/National Research Council, op. cit. 15, p.92.
19. *Independent on Sunday*, 5 May 1991.
20. Strange, op. cit. 1, pp.114–115.
21. Body, R., *Agriculture: The Triumph and The Shame*, Temple Smith, London, 1982, p.5.
22. Pye-Smith, C. and Hall, C. (eds), *The Countryside We Want*, Green Books, Bideford, 1987, p.9.
23. Body, op. cit. 21, p.13.
24. Belden, op. cit. 16, p.4.
25. Belden, op. cit. 16, p.23.
26. Strange op. cit. 1, p.41.
27. Ibid, p.36.
28. Lang, T., *Food Retailing Concentration: Its implications for consumers*, unpublished manuscript, pp.16–17.
29. Hobbelink, H., op. cit. 5, p.47.
30. Ward, N., "A Preliminary analysis of the UK food chain", *Food Policy*, October 1990, pp.439–441.
31. Erlichman, J., *Gluttons for Punishment*, Penguin, Harmondsworth, 1986, pp.68–69.
32. Strange, op. cit. 1, p.41.
33. Heffernan, W.D., "Confidence and Courage in the next Fifty Years", Presidential Address delivered at the Annual Meeting of the Rural Sociological Society in Athens, Georgia, 20 August 1988, p.8.

34. Barnes, P., "The Corporate Invasion", *The Ecologist* 7, No. 6, 1977, p.197.
35. Heffernan op. cit. 33, pp.8–10.
36. Ibid.
37. Ibid.
38. Erlichman, J., "Progress halves chickens' lifespan", *The Guardian*, 15 October 1991, p.4.
39. Lang, T., op. cit. 28, p.5.
40. National Academy of Sciences/National Research Council, op. cit. 15, p.38.
41. Parrish, P. "Wheatarama — A British Farmer's Perspective", *Food Matters Worldwide* 10, p.12.
42. "Canada, Cargill and Free Trade", *Food Matters Worldwide* 10, p.10.
43. Lang, T., op. cit. 28, p.12.
44. Ibid, p.17.
45. Getz, A., Paper given at the Fourth International Permaculture Conference, in Kathmandu, Nepal 10–15 February 1991.
46. Mooney, C., "A healthy diet — who can afford it?", *Food Magazine*, October 1988, p.20.
47. Personal communication from Robin Jenkins in response to first draft.
48. Lang, T., op. cit. 28, p.25.
49. Ibid, p.9.
50. Cowe, R., "Sainsbury and Tesco — are we up to supporting so many superstores?" *The Guardian* 19 March 1991.

## New Barons

1. Commission of the European Communities, *Communication of the Commission to the Council: The Development and Future of the CAP, Reflection Paper of the Commission*, COM (91) 100 Final, Brussels, 1 February 1991.
2. Pye-Smith, C. and Hall, C. (eds), *The Countryside We Want*, Green Books, Bideford, 1987, p.9.
3. Ibid.
4. MacSkimming, D., "Compensation for SSSI restriction nets Scots farmer £0.5m', *Farmers Weekly*, 14 June 1991, p.25.
5. Henkoff, R., "Farmers: No more high on the hog", *Fortune*, 2 December 1991, p.100.
6. National Academy of Sciences/National Research Council, *Alternative Agriculture*, National Academy Press, Washington, DC, 1989, p.129.
7. Body, R., *Farming in the Clouds*, Temple Smith, London, 1984, p.21.
8. National Agricultural Chemicals Association, *Industry Profile Survey 1986*, National Agricultural Chemicals Association, Washington, 1987. Cited in National Academy of Sciences/National Research Council, op. cit. 6, p.44, quoting National Agricultural Chemicals Association, 1987.

9. *Fortune* 22 April 1991.
10. Gips, T., *Breaking the Pesticide Habit: Alternatives to 12 Hazardous Pesticides*, International Alliance for Sustainable Agriculture, Publication No. 1987-1, Minnesota, 1987, p.299.
11. Figure provided by Bill Barclay, Pesticides Project, Greenpeace International, USA in response to draft.
12. "The Food and Drink Market", *Food From Britain Annual Report*, 1989/90.
13. "Focus on Europe", *The Grocer*, 9 June 1990, p.34.
14. Ibid.
15. Ibid.
16. Hobbelink, H., *Biotechnology and the Future of World Agriculture*, Zed Books, London, 1991, p.47.
17. Heffernan, W.D., *Confidence and Courage in the next Fifty Years*, Presidential Address delivered at the Annual Meeting of the Rural Sociological Society in Athens, Georgia, 20 August 1988, p.18.
18. Strange, M., *Family Farming: A New Economic Vision*, University of Nebraska Press and Institute of Food and Development Policy, Lincoln, London, San Francisco, 1988, p.39.
19. Body, R., *Our Food, Our Land: Why contemporary farming practices must change*, Rider, London, 1991, p.139.
20. Crossley, G., "Farmers Weekly Adviser Survey", *Farmers Weekly*, 6 January 1984.
21. Van Den Bosch, R., *The Pesticide Conspiracy*, Prism Press, Dorchester, 1980, p.132.
22. Harvey, G., "Bias in the agricultural press", *New Farmer and Grower* 27 (Summer 1990), p.12.
23. Hobbelink, H., op. cit. 16, p.39.
24. Strange, M., op. cit. 18, p.217.
25. Hobbelink, H., op. cit. 16, p.39.
26. Rose, C., *The Dirty Man of Europe*, Simon and Schuster, London, 1990, pp.234–7.
27. Rose, C., "Pesticides: An Industry out of Control", in Goldsmith, E. and Hildyard, N. (eds), *Green Britain or Industrial Wasteland*, Polity/Blackwell, Cambridge, p.162.

## Undermining Alternatives

1. National Academy of Sciences/National Research Council, *Alternative Agriculture*, National Academy Press, Washington, DC, 1989, p.10.
2. Ibid, p.69.
3. Cited in E. Goldsmith, *Agroecosystems and their Destruction*, unpublished manuscript, 1990.

4. Agriculture and Food Research Council, *Agriculture and Food Research Council Corporate Plan 1988–1993*, HMSO, London, 1988.
5. Throughout the 1980s, officials repeatedly stressed that they would be quite happy to carry out research into organic farming if the organic movement provided the funds.
6. Briggs, S., "Silent Spring: The View from 1990", *The Ecologist*, Vol. 20, No. 2, March/April 1990.
7. Snell, P., "Pesticide Regulation in Britain", *The Ecologist*, Vol. 20, No. 2, March/April 1990.
8. Information put out by the Soil Association, British Organic Farmers and the Organic Growers Association during the late 1980s.
9. Lane, N., "Scab Alternative", *New Farmer and Grower* 7, (Summer 1985), p.34.
10. National Academy of Sciences/National Research Council, op. cit. 1, p.12.
11. Ibid, p.83.
12. Fitzsimmons, J., "Green Consumerism: An inherent contradiction?" Paper presented to Ecopolitics V conference, University of NSW, Sydney, Australia, April 1991.
13. Hornsby, M., "Dairy farmers find their free trade initiative going sour', *The Times* 8 November 1991, p.8.
14. Norman, B., "Making the Grade", *New Farmer and Grower* 26, pp.24–27.
15. Lang, T., "Food Retailing Concentration: Its implications for consumers", unpublished manuscript 1991.
16. "Supermarkets stem stock cash lifelines", *Farmers Weekly*, 7 December 1990, p.14.

## Mainstream Responses

1. House of Lords Select Committee Report "Development and Future of the Common Agricultural Policy", HL Paper 79-1, HMSO, London, 1991.
2. Council for the Protection of Rural England, *Future Harvests*, Council for the Protection of Rural England, London, 1990.
3. Soil Association, *Guidelines for Conservation*, Soil Association, Bristol, 1989, p.3.
4. The decision by Dorset County Council to allow the building of houses on an SSSI caused an outcry from environmentalists and several national environmental bodies were moved to protest. The issue was reported in the local and national press.
5. Ministry of Agriculture, Fisheries and Food, Northern Ireland Office, Scottish Office and Welsh Office, *Farming U.K.*, HMSO, London, 1987, p.37.

6. Body, R., *Our Food, Our Land: why contemporary farming practices must change*, Rider, London, 1991, p.289.
7. Rose, C., *The Dirty Man of Europe: The Great British Pollution Scandal*, Simon and Schuster, London, 1990, pp.80–85.
8. Soil Association, "The Links between Organic Farming and nature conservation: A response to 'Future Harvests' published by the Council for the Protection of Rural England", Soil Association, Bristol, March, 1991.
9. "Senate Exposé: 400% increase in bacterial contamination of mass-produced chickens", draft of an article for The Animal Welfare Institute Quarterly, USA.
10. The London Food Commission, *Food Adulteration and how to beat it*, Unwin, London, 1988, p.238.
11. Ibid, p.241.
12. Piccioni, R., "Food Irradiation: Contaminating Our Food", *The Ecologist*, Vol. 18, Nos. 2/3, 1988, pp.48–55.

## The Real Agenda

1. Task Force Report on the Environment and the Internal Market, *"1992" The Environmental Dimension*, Task Force Environment and the Internal Market and Economica Verlag, Bonn, p.109.
2. The Draft Final Act, GATT Trade Negotiation Committee, MTN.TNC/W/ FA, 20th December 1991, Geneva, GATT.
3. Ritchie, M., "GATT, Agriculture and the Environment", *The Ecologist*, Vol. 20, No. 6, November/December 1990, pp.214–220.
4. Participants list, Codex Alimentarius Commission Pesticides Residues Committee, 15–19 April 1991, Rome.
5. Ritchie, M., op. cit. 3, pp.214–220.
6. Ibid, p.216.
7. Ibid.
8. Lang, T., *Food fit for the world?: How the GATT food trade talks challenge public health, the environment and the citizen*, SAFE Alliance and Public Health Alliance, London, March, 1992, pp.27–28.
9. Ibid.
10. Joint press release by 15 NGOs, "GATT Tuna–Dolphin Decision: Information Packet", Public Citizen, 1991.
11. Ibid.
12. Ibid.
13. Hindmarsh, R. "The Flawed 'Sustainable' Promise of Genetic Engineering", *The Ecologist*, 21, No. 5, p.200.
14. Ibid, p.198.

15. Ibid, p.203.
16. Ibid, p.196.
17. Ibid, pp.198–9.
18. Hatchwell, P., "Opening Pandora's Box", *The Ecologist*, Vol. 19, No. 4 July/August 1989, p.136.
19. Hindmarsh, R., Unedited version of "The Flawed 'Sustainable' Promise of Genetic Engineering", op. cit. 13. This quote was cut from published version.

## Movements for Change

1. Jackson, W., Berry, W. and Colman, B. (eds), *Meeting the Expectations of the Land: Essays in Sustainable Agriculture and Stewardship*, North Point Press, San Francisco, 1984, p.x.
2. Perlas, N., *The Sustainable Agriculture Movement: Healing Human Societies and the Earth with a New Science and Philosophy of Nature*, Center for Alternative Development Initiatives: Occasional Paper No. 1, undated.
3. Quoted in Lampkin, N., *Organic Farming*, Farming Press, Ipswich, 1990, p.4.
4. See the *Soil Association Standards for Organic Agriculture*, Soil Association, Bristol, 1989.
5. United States Department of Agriculture, *Report and Recommendations on Organic Farming*, USDA, USA, 1980, p.xii.
6. National Academy of Sciences/National Research Council, *Alternative Agriculture*, National Academy Press, Washington, DC, 1989, p.8.
7. Lampkin, op. cit. 3, p.584.
8. Grateful thanks to Peter Bane, Permaculture Activist, Route 1, Box 38, Primm Springs, TN 38476, USA and George Sobol, Permaculture Association (Britain), P.O. Box 1, Buckfastleigh, Devon, UK for providing much of the information for the section on permaculture.
9. Personal communication from Peter Bane, Permaculture Activist, Hawaii, 23 August 1991.
10. Ibid.
11. Grateful thanks to Bob Waller and David Gordon, 19 Gordon Road, Clifton, Bristol, UK for providing most of the information for this section.
12. For example Ron Lee at Cadbury Court Farm, Clevedon; Arthur Hollins at Fordhall Farm, Market Drayton and others, contact David Gordon (11 above) for further information.
13. The Men of the Trees, *The Men of the Trees Tree Farm Project*, The Men of the Trees, Australia, March 1991, p.2.
14. *Scotland's Forest Charter, A Contribution from NGOs in Scotland to the United Nations Convention on World Forests*, February 1991, Third Draft. Available from: Reforesting Scotland, Duartbeg, Scourie, Sutherland,

## REFERENCES

Scotland. See also *A Forest for Scotland: A discussion paper on forest policy*, Scottish Wildlife and Countryside Link, Perth, 1992.

15. Groh, T.M. and McFadden, S.H., *Farms of Tomorrow: Community supported farms, farm supported communities*, Bio-Dynamic Farming and Gardening Association, Kimberton, 1990.

16. Paper on "Community Supported Agriculture" by Arthur Getz at Fourth International Permaculture Conference, Nepal, 10–15 February 1991.

17. Cook, J., "Farm Fresh", *Harrowsmith Country Life*, May/June 1990, pp. 53–57.

18. Ibid.

19. Personal communication from Robyn Van En, Indian Line Farm, Mass, USA (undated) September 1991.

20. Ibid.

21. Ibid.

22. Groh, T.M. and MacFadden, S.H., op. cit. 15, pp.6–7.

23. *The Seikatsu Club*, The Seikatsu Club Consumers Co-operative, Tokyo, 1988/9.

24. Eronn, R., *Ecological Living in Sweden — Ideas and Practical Experience*, The Swedish Institute, Stockholm, (undated) 1990 or 1991.

25. Paper by Tony Andersenn on "Permaculture in the Urban Setting" at Fourth International Permaculture Conference, Nepal, 10–15 February 1991.

26. Paper by Max O. Lindegger on "Village Design" at Fourth International Permaculture Conference, Nepal, 10–15 February 1991.

27. Information provided by Professor George Chan, Guangdon, China.

28. Strange, M., *Family Farming: A New Economic Vision*, University of Nebraska Press and Institute of Food and Development Policy, Lincoln, London, San Francisco, 1988, p.276.

29. Ibid, p.277.

30. Charter reproduced in The London Food Commission, *Food Adulteration and how to beat it*, Unwin, London, 1988, p.xix.

31. *Declaration of the Meeting of Ecological Consumers' Groups*, Bonn, 20–22 April 1990.

32. Over fifteen groups ranging from the National Farmers Union to the National Federation of Women's Institutes, from the Vegetarian Society to Compassion in World Farming were united in their opposition to the licensing of BST in Europe.

33. SAFE, Draft Document on CAP Reform, unpublished, 1991.

34. Action for a Sustainable Agriculture Policy (ASAP) Campaign Statement, SAFE, London, 1991. Available from: SAFE, 21, Tower Street, London, WC2H 9NS.

35. SAFE, op. cit. 33.

## New Paths

1. Strange, M., *Family Farming: A New Economic Vision*, University of · Nebraska Press and Institute of Food and Development Policy, Lincoln, London, San Francisco, 1988, p.288.

# Index

additives, 28
advertising, 78–9
advisory services, 78
Agricultural Development and
    Advisory Services (ADAS), 78
Agriculture Act (1957), 43–4
Agriculture and Food Research
    Council (AFRC), 85
agrochemicals, 9, 10, 22, 61–3, 75,
    78–9
    see also fertilisers; herbicides;
    pesticides
Areas of Special Scientific Interest
    (ASSIs), 21

Bane, Peter, 121
Barenburg Seeds, 63
bargaining power, 70–3
battery farms, 31–3
Berry, Wendell, 8, 114
biopesticides, 112
    see also pesticides
biotechnology, 110–13
    see also genetic engineering
birds, 22
Body, Richard, 77–8
Bolivia, 35
bovine somatotropin (BST), 33–4,
    102, 139, 141
bovine spongiform encephalopathy
    (BSE), 102

Brazil, 35
Brekilien, Yann, 47, 48
Britain, 42–5
Britten, Barbara, 109
Buccleigh, Duke of, 12
Buschberghof community, 131–3
butterflies, 21
Buxted Poultry, 69

Caillot, Simonne, 47–9
capital costs, 11
carcinogens, 30
Cargill Corporation, 71
Center for Rural Studies, 66
Central Rocky Mountain
    Permaculture, 122
Centre for Rural Affairs, 139
cereals, 9, 16
chemicals, see agrochemicals;
    fertilisers; herbicides; pesticides
Ciba-Geigy, 64
Codex Alimentarius, 82, 108–9
commodity, land as, 12–13
Community Nutrition Institute, 110
community supported agriculture,
    129–37
Consolidated Goldfields, 12
consumer groups, 139–40
contract farming, 69
cosmetic standards, 87
Countryside Commission, 11

crop rotation, 116
Culm Meadows, 20
Czechoslovakia, 24–5

Daimiel wetland site, 21–2
Dalgety-Spillars, 64, 68
Daylay Eggs, 69
DDT, 30
debt, 65–6
Defenders of Wildlife, 110
*dehesa* management, 52–3, 54
Denmark, 138
Department of the Environment, 21
dependency, 60–5
Devon, 20
dolphins, 109
Donana National Park (Spain), 21
Dunkel, Arthur, 107

EC, 16–17, 21, 22, 50, 51
    Common Agricultural Policy
        (CAP), 36–7, 44–5, 46, 74, 105
    Drinking Water Directive, 100
    Environmental Directorate, 54
eco-villages, 137–8
Ecological Consumers Groups, 140
efficiency, myth of, 15–17
employment, agricultural, 11–12
environmental degradation, 19–27,
    96–7
environmental groups, 139–40
Environmental Protection Agency, 86
Environmentally Sensitive Areas
    (ESAs), 99–100
erosion, 22–3, 55–6, 127
ethylene dibromide (EBD), 24
European Ecological Consumers
    Coordination, 140
extensification schemes, 101–2
Extremadura, 53, 54

factory farming, 31–3
farm supply industry, 75
farmer–consumer co-partnerships,
    134–6
farmers leaving land, 11–12
farms, large, 16–17, 74–5
fertilisers, 20, 22, 38, 61
fields, ridging, 19–20
Fitzgerald, John, 110
foggage farming, 127
Food and Environment Act (1985), 81
Food Commission, *see* London Food
    Commission
food dumping, 37
food industry, 76
    corporate control of, 68–70
food irradiation, 139
food labelling, 29
food poisoning, 103–4
food quality, 27–31, 102–4
Food Quality Charter, 139
forest(ry), 54, 128–9
Fowler, Cary, 60, 65
France, 27, 45–9
Friends of the Earth, 19, 26, 100

Game Conservancy Trust, 19
Garst Seeds, 63
General Agreement on Tariffs and
    Trade (GATT), 37, 106–10
genetic engineering, 33–4
    *see also* biotechnology
Genetics Resources Action
    International (GRAIN), 68
global integration of agriculture, 34–7
global warming, 38–9
Gloucestershire, 20
Greenpeace USA, 108
Groh, Christina, 133
Groh, Trauger, 134
groundwater depletion, 25–6

Gummer, John, 41, 88
Gwynedd, 18

habitats, loss of, 19–22
Harvey, Graham, 79
Hatchwell, Paul, 112
health, threats to, 19
hedgerows, 19
Heffernan, Professor, 70, 76
herbicides, 111
Hillsdown Holdings, 69
Hindmarsh, R., 111, 113
Hobbelink, Henk, 68, 79–80
Holland, 24
House of Lords Select Committee, 19
Hudson–Mohawk community farm, 130
hypermarkets, 73
    see also supermarkets

ICI, 63, 64, 75
income support, 74
industry–university contracts, 80
International Federation of Organic
    Agriculture Movements, 117
irrigation, 24, 53–4

Japanese farmer–consumer co-
    partnerships, 134–6

Kite's Nest farm, 118–20

labelling, food, 103
land amalgamation (Spain), 54
land holdings concentration, 66–8
land trusts, 138–9
Lang, Tim, 27
Leonard, Rodney E., 110
lobbying, 82
London Food Commission, 27, 28, 30, 139

Lowe, Philip, 44
lowland areas, 20–1

MacSharry, Ray, 41, 45
manure, 36
marketing structures, 87–8
mechanisation, 9, 10
Mediterranean Wetland (MedWet)
    Forum, 22
Metro Group, 76
Mexico, 109
Milk Corporation (New Zealand),
    87–8
Milk Marketing Board (MMB), 88
milk pasteurisation, 86
Ministry of Agriculture, Fisheries and
    Food (MAFF), 19, 30, 85, 86, 90,
    92–3
Minnesota, 23
Miyoshi Village Co-partnership, 135
Mollison, Bill, 121
monocultures, 15, 16
Mooney, Pat, 60, 65

National Academy of Sciences (USA),
    56–7, 65, 84, 120
National Agricultural Advisory
    Service, 43
National Farmers Union, 19
Nebraska, 57
Netherlands, 36
nitrates, 26, 27, 100–1
Nitrate Sensitive Areas (NSAs),
    26–7, 100–1
Northumberland, Duke of, 12

Ogallala aquifer, 26
organic farming, 115–16, 117–21
Osentowski, Jerome, 122
ozone depletion, 39

Parrish, Peter, 71
paving over, 37–8
Perlas, Nicanor, 114
permaculture, 121–6
permanent pasture systems, 126–8
Pesticide Safety Precaution Scheme (PSPS), 81–2
pesticides, 19, 20, 26, 38, 61–3, 75, 140
  biopesticides, 112
  in food, 29–31
Pesticides Action Network, 140
pig industry, 35
Pioneer Hi-Bred, 64
Plant Breeding Institute, 63
power, issue of, 146–7
price support, 98
processed foods, 27–8
producer–consumer groups, 134–6
Purdey, Mark, 90–4

Rank Hovis McDougal, 63
reafforestation, 54
regulations, 28–9, 86–8
*remembrement* policy, 47, 48
research, control of, 79–81
research bias, 84–6
Rio Tinto Zinc, 12
Rural Advancement Fund International, 60
rural dislocation, 5, 18

SAFE, *see* Sustainable Agriculture, Food and Environment alliance
Sainsbury, 76
salinization, 23–4
salmonella, 32, 88, 102, 103
San Joaquin Valley (California), 25
Scottish Forest Charter, 128–9
Scottish Highlands, 18
Seikatsu Club, 134–5
set-aside schemes, 97

sheep dips, 19, 87
Shell, 64
Sites of Special Scientific Interest (SSSIs), 21, 98–9
Snell, Peter, 31
Société Européene de Semences (SES), 63
Soil Association, 23, 87, 101
soil compaction, 23
soil erosion, 22–3, 55–6, 127
Solkoff, Joel, 85
soybeans, 35
Spain, 18, 21, 49–56
Strange, Marty, 66, 77, 139
subsidies, 16, 17, 43, 83–4, 97–8
supermarkets, 7, 68, 71–2, 76, 89–90
surpluses, 95–6
'sustainable' agriculture, 5, 15, 40
Sustainable Agriculture, Food and Environment (SAFE) alliance, 141–2
Sweden, 137–8

Texas, 25
Thames Valley, 26
Third World countries, 5, 10
toxic pollutants, 24–5
tuna fishing, 109, 141
Turton, Christopher, 70
'two-track' agriculture, 105

UN Food and Agriculture Association (FAO), 36, 108
Unilever, 63, 68
universities, grants to, 80
upland areas, 20
upland farms, 11–12
USA, 25, 56–7
  Environmental Protection Agency, 30, 108
  factory farming, 32–3

Marine Mammal Protection Act, 109

National Academy of Sciences, 56–7, 65, 84, 120

Tax Reform Act, 57

Van En, Robyn, 131

warble flies, 90–1
water pollution, 26–7

waterlogging, 23–4
weed control, 116
wetlands, 21–2
wheat, 9
wildlife, loss of, 19–22
women in farming, 13–14
workforce, agricultural, 11–12

'Young Leaf Society', 136
Young, Richard, 120

For Product Safety Concerns and Information please contact our EU representative GPSR@taylorandfrancis.com Taylor & Francis Verlag GmbH, Kaufingerstraße 24, 80331 München, Germany

Printed and bound by CPI Group (UK) Ltd, Croydon, CR0 4YY

01/05/2025

01858351-0014